Blame Cokey

A LAWYER'S TALE

BILL BLACKBURN

Blame Cokey

A LAWYER'S TALE

For Garry Hunt

Bill Blackburn

January 2003

LP

LEAD PUBLISHING

2002

This edition first published in 2002 by
LEAD Limited
PO Box 35435
London NW8 9YE

email: leadpublishing@msn.com
www.leadpublishing.co.uk

1 3 5 7 9 8 6 4 2

© W. H. Blackburn 2002

A CIP catalogue record for this title is
available from the British Library

ISBN 0 9542225 0 4

Designed and typeset in Albertina at Libanus Press, Marlborough

Printed and bound in Great Britain by
B·A·S Printers Ltd, Over Wallop

For Alexander and Jimmy
and
in memory of Pitche

Pitche

FOREWORD

This memoir was my son Alexander's idea. I wrote it during 2001, when I was recovering from an operation. He and his brother Jimmy had often commented about how little they knew of my origins and early life. Enforced idleness provided an opportunity to put this right. At first, I had expected to write just a few pages of notes, but *Blame Cokey* rapidly took on a life of its own, and is now the length of a short novel. Friends and family assure me that it is also a half-decent read, at least for those with an interest in the subject matter. Several of the anecdotes still amuse me, for one.

The book, as it has become, was written for the entertainment and edification of friends and family. For any of my later descendants, it may also be useful for the record, as every family has its enthusiasts for rooting out the doings of ancestors. If it turns out that *Blame Cokey* has a wider appeal and you know me, or the family, less well, you may wish to know a little more before deciding whether to read on.

As memoirs go, *Blame Cokey* is no tale of heroism or achievement beyond the dreams of ordinary mortals. This is the story of a boy born in Liverpool in the high and far off 1930s, whose journey through the twentieth century, now continuing into the twenty-first, had some distinctly unusual twists and turns along the way. Most importantly, the boy became a man who knew how to have a good time, frequently did, and continues to do so.

Some of the fruits of the journey are in the family tree – my grandchildren and step-grandchildren embrace Danish, French, Hungarian, Mexican and Peruvian origins, not to mention English, Irish, Scottish and Welsh. My friends and associates are scattered across the globe, ranging from the glitterati to the down-right disreputable. I even have some claim to be (nearly) among the great and the good – a Legion of Honour graces my lapel, and there is an OBE in the cupboard for dressing up.

Moving from the sublime to the respectable, I am to this day a director of a building society and I was a pillar of the Law Society. I am, or was, no mean golfer and play devious hands of bridge and poker, if the stakes are attractive. As well as enjoying more than my fair share of love and fun, I am no stranger to loss and pain.

All this, and more, awaits you over the next 35,000 words. I enjoyed writing them. My sons now know all they wanted, with brass knobs on. Over to you . . .

ACKNOWLEDGMENTS

For reminiscences of the early years, I have relied on my sister Joan's memory. Pegi Alexander, Marjory Blackburn, Vida Lloyd-Jones and Robert Oldfield added their recollections. John Guy, archivist at the library of the University of Wales, provided information about Welsh clergy, as did Michael Swales, the secretary of the Old Denstonians. Derek and Nancy Wise commented on our time together in Paris. I had enjoyable meetings with Hamish Adamson, recalling Law Society international events. John Hayes, John Randall and John Young helped put my views of the Law Society into perspective, but those views remain entirely my own. Sir Edwin Nixon, Duncan Campbell and John Drake read and commented on the IBM chapters. Tom Tickell and Paul Wheeler, who both live by the pen, advised on content and presentation. Koukla, my sister-in-law, encouraged me. James Tickell, my stepson, is responsible for both the title and the foreword. I am grateful to them all. Chloë, my wife, read the draft several times, and wielded her red pencil without restraint.

CHAPTER 1

Not a drop of English blood

My name is William Howard Blackburn. I have been married twice, first to Marie-Thérèse (Pitche) Dorange, the mother of my two sons, Alexander and James, and secondly to her great friend, Chloë Gunn. To many I am Bill, but my mother called me Billie. I was born in Liverpool on 23 December 1932, and my parents named me in memory of my father's recently deceased brother. I arrived late in my parents' marriage. My mother was forty-five and my father a couple of years older. I had two sisters, Margaret (Peggy) and Joan, and they were respectively fourteen and nine when I was born. These were the Depression years, but we did not suffer any hardship. My father, Tom Blackburn, was blue-eyed, thick-lipped, tall and handsome. He had beautiful soft hair that he washed every day and kept very short – almost crew cut. His family was Northern Irish, of Presbyterian farming settler stock, and my mother, Elizabeth (Lily) Jones, was Welsh, a dark-haired beauty from Llandudno. She was known as Lily, because her brother Victor was not, as a child, capable of pronouncing Elizabeth.

The Welsh dragons

My mother's family was entirely Welsh and its origins were in the remote Lleyn peninsula in Caernarfonshire. My mother's maternal grandmother, Catrin, was born around 1830, and spoke only Welsh. Her husband, William Williams, was a weaver. The family legend is that he would go off to the local town, Pwllheli, to sell his cloth and come back with a sack full of books. Their house in the village of

Llaniestyn was called Tan-Yr-Ardd. My mother's other grandmother, Elizabeth Jones, lived at Hendy, Llandegwning, which is near Hell's Mouth Bay at the end of the Lleyn.

My mother's mother, Margaret, died aged ninety-three, in September 1948. I remember her being beautifully and neatly dressed in black, with a pretty brooch at her neck. She had been a lady's maid and was companion to Lady Jones-Parry of Madryn Castle near Pwllheli. The baronetcy, created in 1886,[1] was extinguished on Sir Thomas's death in 1891, because the Jones-Parrys were childless. According to a copy of *Burke's Peerage* for 1911, which I have, Lady Jones-Parry was then still alive and living in Wilton Place, Belgravia.

Three of my grandmother's four brothers, William, Griffith and Richard, became Anglican clergymen. The other brother, Robert, was a farmer, but I am told that he enjoyed painting more than farming. Red-headed William was born in 1848 and died in 1930. He went to Llaniestyn National School, entered St David's College, Lampeter, as a scholar and became the Dean of the Cathedral at St David's in Pembrokeshire. William started as an evangelical and ended up a high Anglican, introducing vestments and candles. He is a significant figure in the history of the Cathedral and was the man who 're-discovered' the relics of St David. These have now proved, on analysis, to be bones of a later date. There is a plaque in his memory at St David's Cathedral.

The second brother, Griffith, was born in 1860 and educated at Denstone College, Uttoxeter in Staffordshire, a Woodard School. He entered St David's College, Lampeter in 1879 and became a priest in 1884. He was Rector of Pentrevoelas and a rural dean. According to family legend, the Jones-Parrys paid for the education of the boys, but it is more likely that they obtained bursaries. The Woodard Foundation is a charity whose object is the formation of ministers for the Anglican Church. On the recommendation of parish clergy, Denstone would provide scholarships for

1 Sir Thomas Love Duncombe Jones-Parry must be the only baronet to have been sentenced to death by firing squad. This happened in Spain in 1859, when a Spanish Court condemned him for assault- ing a sentry at La Linea. Queen Isabella pardoned him. She was under the misapprehension that he was the son of the British General Sir Love Parry, who had fought with Wellington in Spain.

bright boys destined for the church. Griffith went to Denstone in 1874, the school having opened the previous year. He had a son, Howard Glynne Williams, who also went to Denstone. He was awarded exhibitions to both Selwyn and St Catherine's Colleges, Cambridge, and took his degree at St Catherine's in 1913. He was commissioned in the army, wounded at Salonika and died of his wounds in 1917.

My grandmother, Margaret, had travelled on the Continent with her mistress and she knew 'how things should be done'. She married the coachman of Madryn

Grandmother Nain

Castle, William Jones, and, when she left the employ of the Jones-Parrys, she and her husband set up a cab business in Llandudno. They had about fifteen horse cabs, running people from the station to their hotels and on holiday outings. The first coach and the house in Llandudno were gifts of the Jones-Parrys. Lady Jones-Parry was always calling Margaret back to the castle, but after some years William decreed that she should return there no more. William and Margaret spoke Welsh together. We knew them as Nain and Taid, meaning grandmother and grandfather in Welsh. They are buried in the family grave in the churchyard at St Tudno's Church on the Great Orme overlooking the sea, a most romantic spot.

My mother, Elizabeth, was one of a family of seven. Her eldest brother, Victor, was a Chief Petty Officer in the Navy and gunfire at Jutland had rendered him deaf. He had one son, also Victor, who was drowned in the 1939–45 War when on his way to join his ship as a seaman in the Merchant Marine. Like many sailors, Uncle Victor was good with his hands. He made me a beautiful model yacht, which I used to sail on a pond specially built for model boats on the West Shore in Llandudno. I can still hear the slap of the small waves on the side of the pond in the ever-present wind. Another brother, Richard, died in 1916 of pneumonia while on leave from the army. He was given a military funeral in Llandudno. This was a large affair, the first such event in the town. The third brother, Griffith, took over the family taxi business and had two children, John and William. Griffith and his wife died early and my mother became legal guardian to the two boys, although Ellen, my mother's sister, who was on the spot, carried out the day-to-day duties. John joined the RAF and then worked for the Post Office as a technician. William, called Billy, was a severe epileptic and worked as a gardener.

Mother's sister Ellen stayed at home to look after my grandmother. She had been engaged, but her fiancé died just after the 1914–18 war. The second sister, Sarah, married David Thomas-Jones, a clergyman from Cardiganshire, who became the vicar of Caernarfon and a canon of Bangor Cathedral. I remember Uncle David as a rotund man, reading in his large study in the vicarage in Caernarfon, sitting in a leather armchair, surrounded by books and smoking his pipe. He had a chair that had been presented to him at the National Eisteddfod, the Welsh Folk Festival. He often preached in Welsh. He must have been an evangelical rather than a high church Anglican because I remember being surprised as a little boy to hear him express anti-Catholic opinions. He served in the 1914–18 War with the Welch Regiment as a chaplain in the Palestine Campaign. He and Sarah had three girls, Vida, Pegi and Ann. My mother's third and youngest sister, Mary, married Will Davies, who became the Midland Bank manager in Presteigne, Radnorshire. Their only child Brenda married, and then divorced, Richard Shipton and she now lives in Bridport, Dorset. Brenda and Richard had two children, Julia and Peter.

Llandudno, where my maternal grandparents lived, is a seaside resort, beautifully situated between two small mountains, the Great and the Little Orme. The Great Orme has steep cliffs down to the sea that are a nesting site for thousands of seabirds; their cries and the smell of the sea air are strong memories. The local boys risked their lives on the cliffs collecting gulls' eggs and I regretted that I was too young to join them. The town has sea on both sides and a lovely Victorian Pier. The view from the West Shore is over the mountains of Snowdonia. My grandparents' house was called Combermere. It was situated on Deganwy Avenue, near the centre of town and opposite the back of the recently built Odeon Cinema, which had previously been the site of a market garden. The house was large enough for all the family and for bed and breakfast guests in the season, although Uncle Griffith sometimes had to sleep in the garden shed to make room. There were mains water, gas and electricity and I remember the soft light of the remaining gas mantle lights, and the large basins and jugs in the bedrooms, filled with hot water every morning.

The family lived in the kitchen, which was in the basement, sitting around the large table. Above the door there was a sign saying, 'God is Master of this House'. My grandfather did not agree with the sentiment and arranged for the notice to disappear. There was a dark larder with a grille in the wall in which food was placed to keep cool. The knives were not stainless steel. There was a knife-cleaning machine into which one placed them, turning the handle to keep the steel polished. This was one of my chores when I went to stay. On Saturday mornings I would go to the Odeon with all the other children from the town for a matinée. They showed serials which went on from week to week, always stopping at the most exciting point with, for example, the heroine tied down to the track and a train coming. I was always disappointed at missing the next episode when I had to go home to Liverpool. There were trams to get around Llandudno, which is fairly flat, and a cable tram that went to the top of the Great Orme. I would go up the Orme and roam for miles. Uncle Victor had a small boat and we would go out to fish for mackerel and codlings. If he had not caught any fish, I would be sent to the promenade on the sea front to buy supper from the local fishermen. This was my first experience of 'wallet' fishing.

Aunt Mary and Uncle Will lived in Presteigne, Radnorshire. They had a house giving directly on to the road, with a big garden behind. As I have said, Uncle Will was the local bank manager, and he would take me into the bank with him. This did not last long because I stuck my nose into the books and was heard to say about someone in the street, 'That is Mr Jones – do you know that he only has £50 in his account?' It was the first time that I came across stinginess: I was not allowed both butter and jam on the bread at teatime and my aunt would save pound notes by placing them between the leaves of books. Every afternoon, we would go for a long walk with the dog, choosing a different route each day through the beautiful surrounding countryside.

The red hand of Ulster

My father's parents were Ulster Protestants from the countryside near Omagh, County Tyrone. His father, John Blackburn, came from Clogher. His mother, another Elizabeth, was born Johnston and her grandparents' farm at Drumquin was called Killen. Her father was a younger son who came to Liverpool and started a business of grocers' shops and wholesale food imported from Ireland. In its heyday there were thirteen shops. John Blackburn, my grandfather, was taken into the business when he married Elizabeth Johnston and it was renamed 'Johnston & Blackburn'.

They had three children of which my father, Thomas Cather Johnston Blackburn, was the eldest. The younger brother was William Howard and the only girl was Jean. The boys went to school at the Liverpool Collegiate School opposite a Roman Catholic school, St Francis Xavier. Father would steal a cap from a Catholic boy and then behave badly so that the boys of St Francis Xavier would be blamed. His brother, William Howard, went on to Christ's College, Cambridge, qualified as a doctor at Bart's Hospital in London and ended up in the public health sector working as the Medical Officer of Health in Lowestoft. I have his parchment Public Health Diploma, awarded by Cambridge University. Father's sister married an accountant, Sidney Colvin. The Colvin children were Anthony, Margaret and Jean. Anthony became an accountant like his father. Margaret died young in a bicycle accident. Jean married and went to live in South Africa. I believe that there are still Colvin cousins, the children of Anthony, living on the Wirral peninsular, across the Mersey River from Liverpool.

My father did not get along at all well with his father. Their relationship was so bad that he was disinherited and in fact my grandfather completely cut both my

The Blackburn house today in Northern Ireland

father, and his sister Jean, out of his will. I sometimes wonder what either had done to deserve such treatment. John Blackburn died a fairly rich man, leaving £21,000 in 1930, the equivalent of over £800,000 today. He left £10,000 to his younger son, William Howard, and the remainder to his brother, Robert Blackburn in Ulster. As my grandfather had married into the Johnston family, this had the effect of transferring Johnston money to the Blackburn family. Sydney Colvin, Jean's husband, wanted my father to join with him in disputing the will. My father refused, and put up the Irish heirs when they came to Liverpool to settle the estate. He took pride in having conducted himself with dignity. Colvin and my father never spoke again.

In the long term, Father did not suffer financially from being disinherited. To express it in modern jargon, it was more of a short-term cash flow problem for him. One of his Johnston uncles, William, known as Gogo, came to stay for three weeks early in my parents' marriage. He remained for thirteen years and then returned to Ireland where he died. Gogo left an estate of £12,000 and made Father his heir. Mother would sometimes grumble that she had done all the work looking after Gogo, but had received nothing in return. I presume that Father did not share the money with my mother. Father then inherited his brother's estate of about the same amount, when he died of tuberculosis in Davos in 1931.

When in the sanatorium in Davos, Uncle William Howard was a fellow patient of Harry Clarke, an Irish artist of considerable talent. He was particularly known for his stained glass and there are fine examples in the chapel of University College, Cork. I have some of his splendid pen and ink drawings, which I picked out of the dustbin: Mother had thrown them out because she considered them pornographic.

On my grandfather's death, Father took over what he could of the family business. He reduced it to seven shops. Even so, having no working capital, he had to borrow the necessary funds to finance the operation. For some years he found life hard. For example, his house in Onslow Road was not immediately fully furnished. Nevertheless, from about the year of my birth, he always had a car. The first was an Austin 12 in fawn and black. Its registration number was LV 271. This seems to indicate that it was the two hundred and seventy-first car in the city. It had tables that folded into the back seats. He was particularly proud of the black German Opel he had at the beginning of the 1939 War. He had to change it because there was strong anti-German feeling and the car kept being vandalised. He also had an early telephone, with the number Anfield 2. He might have had Anfield 1, but Everton Football Club got that.

Father was intelligent. He did the *Telegraph* crossword before breakfast and the one in *The Times* during the day, often finishing it before lunch. He read a lot and was politically engaged in the Social Credit Movement, a political party whose members believed that the economy could be boosted by creating credit. This was a pre-Keynesian economic and political theory and the party actually came to power in Alberta, Canada. It had little chance of success there because it had no control over Canadian national monetary and economic policy. The party was suspected of being close to the Nazi party in its ideas, although it was not anti-Semitic. Some members of the party were even interned at the beginning of the 1939–45 War in the Isle of Man. This did not include Father, but I think that he might have gone to the Isle of Man to see his colleagues because I remember him saying that the place was full of interned Italian waiters and German musicians. He said that the food, service and music were all excellent.

Father seemed to know Shakespeare by heart and he composed poetry, though perhaps I should call it doggerel: it certainly rhymed and had a metre. He quoted both Shakespeare and poetry often and at length. I can hear him now reciting,

> What is this life if, full of care,
> We have no time to stand and stare?
> No time to stand beneath the boughs
> And stare as long as sheep and cows.
> No time to see, when woods we pass,
> Where squirrels hide their nuts in grass.
> No time to see, in broad daylight,

Streams full of stars, like skies at night.

No time to turn at Beauty's glance,

And watch her feet, how they can dance.

No time to wait till her mouth can

Enrich that smile her eyes began.

A poor life this if, full of care,

We have no time to stand and stare.[2]

He could play the piano and sing. I have early memories of being at the piano with him and singing 'Danny Boy' and 'I'll walk beside you through the passing years'. He had secrets from us, his children – one was so well kept that I only learned it in the year 2000. He had been expelled from school for violent behaviour when he threw an inkwell at a teacher in a rage, which could account, at least in part, for his bad relationship with his father.

When he was thrown out of school, his parents made him an apprentice in the family business. This was a punishment. He was made to serve his time as a grocer. There were always a number of apprentices and they lived at the top of the Blackburn family house in Norwood Grove. The apprentices worked on Saturday night in the shops until about eleven o'clock. The shops closed at ten and then they had to clean up. On Sunday, after breakfast, the boys, presumably including Father, had to line up outside the house to be checked for cleanliness. Grandmother then walked them in line to the Presbyterian Church. After lunch, they had to attend Sunday school, and at six o'clock they were lined up again to go to evening service. Father's mother was somewhat of a tartar. She showed this side of her character to Lizzie Deegan, Father's nanny. Lizzie, when she was hired at the age of fourteen, thought that she would make herself useful by rolling up some skeins of wool into balls. My grandmother said that the balls were not perfect and she made Lizzie undo them all and remake the skeins. Then Lizzie had to roll the wool exactly as demonstrated – six turns around the ball, then turn a quarter.

2   W H Davies

Father went off to Canada before the 1914–18 War where he made a living buying shoes in New York and selling them in Western Canada. He returned at the beginning of the war. I do not know whether he returned because of the war or because he wanted to enter the family business – presumably at a more senior level. He met my mother in Llandudno when he went there on holiday and stayed at Combermere as a paying guest.

Father was a sick man. He suffered from duodenal ulcers and was operated on several times to have bits of his stomach removed. He later contracted tuberculosis and, like most men of his generation, he smoked continuously, non-filter Gold Flake cigarettes. He seemed to exist on a diet of steamed fish, tripe and yoghurt, long before yoghurt was common. He would have the culture flown over from France by the Yalacta Company. The yoghurt would then be made in little pots until the culture died out and a new supply had to be flown in. At almost every meal he would eat a tomato. He would place it carefully in a glass of very hot water, so that he could peel it easily. He came home for lunch every day and would often sleep in an armchair in the early afternoon. A couple of times he set the chair on fire with a cigarette. He drank, but never at home or in the middle of the day, stopping at a pub in the evening on the way home. The combination of a reduced stomach and alcohol was not a good one and a little alcohol had a strong effect. He was often drunk when driving the car home, but was only once caught by the police. Even then he was not prosecuted.

The Matriarchy

Mother was very good looking, in a dark-haired, dark-eyed, Welsh way. When she met my father she was already engaged. She wrote her fiancé a letter and posted back the engagement ring in an envelope – not something that one would risk doing today. Then she refused to accept an engagement ring. I remember Father buying her a ruby ring for their fortieth wedding anniversary and saying that it would partially make up for the absence of an engagement ring. Mother had received only a basic education. In fact, the marriage was somewhat of an intellectual mismatch. Father was often short-tempered towards the end of his life, having been, I am told, fun to be with when younger. As she grew older, Mother lost few opportunities to be critical of him, particularly to me, her youngest child. She was, however, motherly and caring. She was proud of being a good housewife and was pathologically clean and tidy. Looking back, I think that she was what one might describe as a 'good plain cook'. I certainly ate everything put in front of me. She even managed to persuade me that rabbit (then cheap) was chicken (then expensive). She had little artistic sense or appreciation, but was well dressed and liked to splash out on a new costume of good quality.

Mother came from a family in which the women considered themselves central and men to be a lesser breed. Marital complicity was a concept totally unknown to her and her sisters: husbands were to be either placated or put upon. She had a good sense of humour. I remember coming home when I was about fifteen. Mother was ironing. A girl had told me that I was attractive. 'Mother,' I said, 'am I handsome?' She put the iron down slowly, looked me up and down and said, 'I'm not sure – but in any event you're not my type.' On another occasion, when Joan came home from school, proud of the fact that she had become the captain of the swimming team, Mother said, 'Oh, you can swim?' If my grandmother had a tendency to return to Madryn Castle, Mother would often make Father angry by going back home to visit her family in Llandudno.

Mother

CHAPTER 2

Cokey

My hair became darker as I got older, but when very young I was a hazel-eyed little boy with blonde hair. I look angelic in the photographs of the time, but my temper was violent. I remember screaming, naked, until I was out of breath. While screaming, I loved making faces in the mirror, to look as angry as possible. My sisters would take off my shoes, to avoid being kicked and to protect the furniture, pick me up, and place me outside the room, or sometimes the house, until I stopped. I was at ease with people from an early age. When four, I had a nice silk suit. On meeting my cousin Vida for the first time, I said, 'I'm Billy and this is my cissy suit.'

An angel? December 1935

My earliest memory is of being on holiday in Wales at Tydweiliog, before the 1939–45 War. I was given a penny for pocket money each day and went to the Post Office to buy a bar of Aero chocolate. We stayed at a cottage called Wenallt, which means White Hill in Welsh. I remember the squealing of the pigs when they were removed for slaughter – they seemed to know that something terrible was about to happen to them. We were well fed from the flock of sheep which grazed in the field at the back of the cottage. Day by day, we would eat our way through a lamb – the two legs, the two shoulders and the chops. The neck and ribs were made into an Irish stew. Then another lamb would be killed. We spent a lot of time on the beach. There was a good deal of driftwood in those days, before the appearance of plastic. We built bonfires and cooked sausages, the original barbecue. We had to be careful to protect the food, because sometimes a pig would come rooting around on the sands.

Evacuation

When war broke out in 1939, my sister Peggy and her boyfriend Ken drove me, in Father's car, to Caernarfon in North Wales to stay with Aunty Sarah and Uncle David. When I woke up next morning I was furious to discover that my sister had gone – owing me sixpence. It was a Sunday morning. At the breakfast table Uncle David gave out sixpences for us to give in the Church collection. 'Sixpence?' said I. 'It's cheaper in Liverpool.'

There were three daughters in the family: Ann, who was my age, and her two elder sisters, Vida and Pegi. The latter qualified as nurses at the Liverpool Royal Infirmary, joined the Queen Alexandra Nursing Corps in the War, and served in India. Vida married Jack Lloyd-Jones, a solicitor. He became the chief legal officer to the development corporation that built the new town of Cwm Bran in South Wales. They had four children: John, Sara, Timothy and Huw. Pegi married a doctor, Ken Alexander, who became a consultant pathologist, and they live in Stratford upon Avon. They have six children: David, Matthew, Mark, Lucy, Sîan and Laura.

The vicarage in Caernarfon became my home for about six months and I went to a Welsh-speaking school with my cousin Ann. Uncle David and Aunty Sarah took me in and treated me as if I was their own son. I still know a few Welsh words and phrases. To this day, I could ask for a newspaper, say good night and good morning or ask you to close the door, all in Welsh. It was important to know some of the language in Wales during and shortly after the War. Many things were in short supply and were kept under shop counters. You could never buy them if you asked in English.

The vicarage was a large Victorian house and extremely untidy. I remember that one sometimes had to clear a space at the kitchen table to be able to sit down to eat. Unlike her sister Lily, Aunty Sarah much preferred playing the piano to housework or cooking. She was quite eccentric, had considerable charm, and was a great deal of fun. She bicycled everywhere and spoke to almost everyone she met. I remember her going to the railway station when Uncle David needed to go to Bangor and holding the train up because he was a little late. The vicarage was situated on the site of a Roman fort, Segontium. We found Roman coins in the garden and played with Roman artefacts. The house has now been pulled down but, opposite, also on the site of the Roman fort, there is an interesting museum.

Ann was my favourite cousin. She moved to London and married Lyle Blenner-hasset de Courcy. When her father died she asked me to advise her about getting an annulment of the marriage. I remember saying it was impossible – effectively she would have to prove her virginity. She surprised me somewhat by saying that she could prove it by medical examination and that she had waited for her father's death to start legal proceedings because she did not want to upset him. I helped her to start the proceedings and her marriage was annulled. Lyle remarried, lives in Bath, and has a stepchild. Ann then married a doctor in private practice in Llandudno, Ian Wynn-Hughes. He was a lovely man, an enthusiastic rugby player and medical officer to the North Wales Air/Sea Rescue Team. They have two children, Claire and Adam. I remember that when I went to visit them they would move back the carpet and produce a bottle from under the floor. This was in case Ian's parents called unexpectedly. The drink had to be hidden because Ian's father was a Methodist preacher and, therefore, strictly teetotal – he retained the illusion that his son never drank alcohol. When very ill, Ian was sent a case of champagne. He drank it, having persuaded his parents that it was a fizzy mouthwash.

The Blitz

The war started quietly, so I returned to Liverpool – just in time for the bombing. I remember the air raids, the nights in the shelter, my father coming into the air-raid shelter in the garden covered in the blood of a neighbour killed by an anti-aircraft shell that fell back to earth. I would get up at dawn and go looking for shrapnel. I was proud of my collection and particularly prized the nose sections of shells and the larger pieces of shell and bomb cases. The bombing of Liverpool was severe. Land mines, dropped by parachute, destroyed groups of houses, and small phosphorous bombs started fires all over the city. I ran wild, playing in abandoned houses and on bombsites.

The house always seemed to be full of young people. It was a rallying point for Peggy's medical student friends and for those of my nurse cousins, Vida and Pegi. I remember being taken to the Far East Restaurant, one of the first Chinese restaurants in England. It always had food during the war, and my first dish was Egg Foo Yong – just an omelette, but an omelette made with fresh eggs was then a rare event. Chicken Chow Mein was another favourite. The Far East did not bother with rations and the Chinese seamen provided food from the ships. I retained a taste for Chinese food and later, when at University, I invited a Portuguese friend, Remy Baradas, to a Chinese restaurant for lunch. I ordered, and he ate what I ordered, but the following week he taught me a lesson I have never forgotten. He invited me back to the same restaurant. He ordered in Chinese and the food was much better. It was superb in fact. When the bill came he disputed it in Chinese and got a substantial discount. He had not said that he was Portuguese from Macao, where his family had lived for hundreds of years.

Food was short and the black market flourished. For example, when staying with Aunty Sarah in Caernarfon, I was sent out to the nearest farms to buy butter. Each farm made and sold its own butter and one could recognise which farm the butter came from by the pattern stamped on the top of the pat. This was black market butter. In Liverpool, a local policeman made and sold cakes. He obtained the ingredients on the black market. Perhaps because my father's office was separate from the warehouse where the food was kept, we respected the rations, although we did buy the policeman's cakes. The Italian prisoners in a nearby camp received good and different rations, including dried fruit and rice. We were able to do exchanges with them. Although I was never hungry during the war, we certainly lacked such things as fruit. We seemed at times to live on dried milk, dried eggs, concentrated orange juice, bread and potatoes. The sausages were mainly filled with bread. There were no oranges or grapefruit and I first saw a banana when the war was over. When the American troops arrived in about 1943, I learned, like other British children, to beg for chocolate and chewing gum saying, 'Any gum, chum?'

First steps towards independence

Father thought that I might become an entrepreneur when it was discovered that I was hiring out my buck rabbit for stud. Mother was deeply shocked that I, at the age of ten, knew all about the breeding process. I spent a lot of time with the local Scout Troop and went camping in North Wales – sometimes cycling seventy miles to get to the campsite with all the kit. After the war, I went on a trip with another scout to Brittany and we walked and camped from St Mâlo to the Mont St Michel. We then caught a bus to Vannes in the South of Brittany and walked and camped around the beautiful Gulf of Morbihan, ending up at Port Navalo. Our map indicated that there was a ferry to the other arm of the gulf at Locmariaquer. Unfortunately, it only worked in the summer season, so we hitched a ride in a fishing boat. The members of the crew were returning from several days at sea and they insisted on taking us for a drink. We all got completely drunk – I for the first time in my life. The captain took us to his home and his wife looked after us until we recovered from our hangovers, which took a few days. It was interesting to share the fisherman's life. Nothing had changed for over a hundred years. His wife cooked over an open fire and the shrimps, for example, were dumped on to the scrubbed table together with the potatoes, after the water had been poured away in the courtyard. We all cut ourselves slices from the loaf, and helped ourselves to salted butter from the large mound placed on the bare table.

My parents arranged for lessons at the local riding school. One day, when I was about twelve or thirteen, I set my pony at a jump. The pony refused, but I went flying over, put out my hand to stop my fall, and stood up with a badly broken arm. I remember the itchy plaster and getting everyone to sign it. I also remember getting into trouble when on a scout camp in North Wales for breaking into a hut in a stone quarry and stealing gelignite, fuse wire and detonators. The police were interested in trying to discover who was blowing up the fish in the park lakes . . . I remember too being reprimanded for throwing stones and breaking the glass of the street lamps. In those days though, if you were of a 'good family', you were not likely to be troubled by the police. You were more likely to be thrashed than to be prosecuted.

Then, as now, I was happy to be alone. Perhaps this is because my sisters were so much older: I was effectively brought up as an only child. Joan was nine when I was born and she loved to look after me as a baby. Even today she refers to me as 'Baby Brother'. Peggy became distinctly less enthusiastic about being seen with me in public when a woman saw her wheeling the pram and took her for my mother. In common with many solitary children, I had an imaginary friend, 'Cokey'. I would have long conversations with Cokey and would blame Cokey if I did anything wrong. I also had an invented language, and my mother would have to ask Joan to interpret what I was saying.

I respect self-reliance and independence, even solitude, as an ideal. In that way, at least, I am a true Anglo-Saxon Protestant. I remember being sent away to the Lleyn peninsula during the war when my father was in hospital for a stomach operation. I lived at a farm on the coast, Tyddyn Mawr, alone with the farmer and his family. There was a privy in the garden, which had running water because it was built over a stream. To flush, one pulled the string that released the small dam created by a wooden board. I remember the strong, but not objectionable, odour. The farmer's English was quite approximate and he would, for example, call a little stream a river. He once spoke of the 'shipses'. The word did not make sense to me and I said that I did not understand him. He became indignant and explained himself by saying, 'Not the shipses on the sea, but the sheepses on the hills.' In effect, I do remember the large number of sheep and also the fields covered with rabbits (it was before myxomatosis almost destroyed them). We would go down to the beach at low tide and the farmer's son would thrust his arm into cracks in the rocks and take out lobsters and large crabs that we would eat for supper. These spots were well known to the farm people, and knowledge of their location must have been passed down from generation to generation. My riding lessons paid off. I was encouraged to hire a horse from the village on a daily basis and would go off exploring, with sandwiches and a bottle of lemonade in a saddlebag for sustenance.

A metaphysical side?

No, being alone has never been difficult for me, but I have never been introspective. Indeed Odile Tirard, a fervent Roman Catholic and friend of Pitche, once said that 'my problem' was that I totally lacked a metaphysical side to my character. Be that as it may, I started in life going to the Anglican Church twice every Sunday. I was baptised and then confirmed. Religion was an unquestioned element in my life for many years and I enjoyed occasionally going to church and listening to evensong on the *Third Programme*. It was with maturity that I began to doubt the Christian faith. Christianity places the human being in the centre of the cosmic stage. This emphasis on the human animal as central to everything became particularly difficult to accept. The idea that we were made in God's image and that Christ was the 'son' of God began to seem more and more ridiculous. So I lost any belief in Christianity and no other faith has taken its place. I am as sure as can be that there is no life after death and doubt whether there is any kind of God, at least any God that a human could comprehend. This is not a rejection of morality, and the Christian doctrine of 'do unto others as you would have done unto you' seems the right way to order one's life. I have, however, no belief in the doctrine of 'turning the other cheek', and I do harbour grudges.

I have met two truly holy men: the Dalai Lama and Cardinal Hume. They both impressed me by their evident goodness and humility. Basil Hume was the Abbot of Ampleforth when Alexander and James were sent there to school. At one time he was spoken of as a potential Pope. I was impressed, when listening to him on Radio 4 after he had been made a Cardinal, by the fact that he never mentioned Jesus Christ or the Virgin Mary. He spoke only of God. I remember expounding my religious doubts to him and saying that it was difficult enough to decide whether one believed in God – from that point on, the choice of faith and then the choice of sect within the chosen faith seemed impossible. He remained calm and smiled. He asked whether I liked wine. I nodded. Did I prefer red or white? 'Red,' I responded. 'Burgundy or Bordeaux?' 'Bordeaux,' was my response. 'There you are,' he said. 'You have it in one, and you must admit that true passion arises in the choice of château.'

This attitude to religion is perhaps inherited from Father. He had been brought up a strict Calvinistic Presbyterian. He never went to the Presbyterian Church, but he supported it financially. At his funeral the Minister spoke warmly of him and clearly knew him well. One day he went to the Anglican Cathedral to pick up my mother at the end of the service. Uncle David was preaching and he had a tendency to get carried away. The Welsh call this emotional religious style the *hwyl*. The service overran and my father stood at the back of the congregation. He was handed a collection plate and he went around, as instructed, taking the collection. When he got to my mother he whispered, 'No show without Punch.' He proceeded up the long aisle of the Cathedral and, with a respectful bow, handed the plate to my astonished uncle. What upset Mother was that he had not bothered to remove his overcoat.

CHAPTER 3

Where did you go to school?

My parents sent me to a nursery school at the age of three and I possess an early, and excellent, report. I read voraciously from an early age and was given an encyclopaedia, entitled *Pictorial Knowledge*, which I devoured. Because of this, I seemed to know everything before it was taught in the first few years of school. When the choice of secondary school came up, there was never any question of going away. I do not know whether this was because of the war – probably not. I went with my parents to Liverpool College, the local public school, for interview and was accepted. Mother, however, did not like the place. There was a picture badly hung on the stairs and she said that she would not send her son somewhere that was not competent enough to hang a picture. Instead, I went to the local grammar school, the Holt, a similar school to Quarry Bank, the Beatles' school.

The Holt was good. It had excellent masters. I remember, in particular, the English master, whose name was Rankin. He was brilliant, and taught us the delights of literature. I am sure that it is because of him that reading became, and remains to this day, my favourite occupation. Strange to think that, without the impetus of Rankin, I might never have developed my passion for Patrick O'Brian, nor have become an enthusiastic member of the Trollope Society. Studies were competitive and there were full sports facilities. The houses were named Troy, Athens, Sparta and Corinth. Each house had its own character. I was in Corinth, the intellectual lot; Sparta was good at games, Athens went for balance, and Troy was arty.

We had an assembly of the whole school each morning. We sang a hymn, the headmaster led us in prayer, and a boy read a chapter of the Bible. Remember, this was a state school. It would be impossible today, but then there were virtually no ethnic minorities except the Chinese near the docks and a black population in the Toxteth district, a virtual ghetto. The school was in effect a Protestant institution with a sprinkling of Jewish pupils. The large Roman Catholic population of Liverpool had its own state-supported schools and was thus completely segregated. I never came across anti-Semitism until many years later in France. This was because we were educated with Jews and liked them. There was, however, a lot of anti-Catholic sentiment among the pupils, because Catholic children, being educated apart, were unknown.

In the sixth form, I improved my Latin by using the vulgate text to follow the Bible reading at morning assembly. The Holt's sixth form results were good, with several boys gaining access to Oxbridge each year. I was awarded a State Scholarship and shared the prize for the best Higher School Certificate. I never took the Scholarship because my father refused to fill in forms revealing his earnings. He must have been doing well at the time because I remember him showing me a £1,000 note, an enormous sum in those days, and explaining that banks used million-pound notes to settle balances between them. The £1,000 note was just like the old fiver, a little smaller, with black script on crinkly heavy white tissue paper.

In the school plays I played only supporting roles. I was not musically gifted, did not sing particularly well and there was no music at home other than the piano and the gramophone. We had full sets of the basic repertory of opera and early on I developed a taste for Puccini and Verdi. I once got into real trouble at school. A pretty young girl was employed as a laboratory assistant and I was caught kissing her. Some of the masters were shocked. I was sent to see the headmaster for punishment. There was talk of being expelled. The headmaster, A G Russell, was a great man and he said that he saw nothing wrong in kissing a pretty girl, but that some of the masters thought it bad for discipline. If he let me off completely, would I please pretend that I had been severely admonished?

When I got to the sixth form, encouraged by my father, I went to Cambridge to be interviewed for Christ's College, which had been my namesake uncle's college.

I was accepted, but was told that, as I was only sixteen, I would have to stay an extra year at school before going up. I was in a hurry to get on with life, so decided to go the Legal Faculty at Liverpool University. I am surprised, when I look back, that my parents and teachers seemed to be happy to let me do as I pleased, without taking a position or giving advice. I sometimes wonder what would have happened to me if I had gone to Cambridge. I would probably have become a barrister: I was always a good debater and speaker. Who knows, I might have become a judge – it has never seemed to me to be an attractive job, having to listen to other lawyers for so long.

I was academically bright and energetic but without any particular gift. I have never been able to draw, and am not interested in science. I was tested by the RAF to measure my mechanical aptitude and discovered that it was high. However, the test measures aptitude and not interest. It seemed natural that the profession for me would be either accountancy or the law. I had no particular gift for figures, so I chose the law and decided to become a solicitor. Given my background and the time, I would have been expected to graduate from Liverpool University, serve articles locally and end up, like most of my contemporaries, a partner in a provincial law firm. It almost happened, but in the end I avoided that destiny.

What position did you play?

My sports prowess was limited. I played soccer and hockey, but not well, and much preferred hockey. Rugby was unknown. At cricket, I found everything too slow and the ball hard. I was, however, quite a good athlete and was nicknamed 'Spider', probably because I was tall and slim – all arms and legs. I was the school champion for the 220 and 440 yards and I was also a good high jumper. In fact I was such a good runner that I was encouraged to join the Liverpool Harriers, the City's running club, to develop my skills, but I never carried on after I left school.

Father played golf occasionally and I was interested in the game. He did not encourage me to play, nor did he ever suggest that I join his club. He never took me on the course nor did he offer to pay for any lessons. I would borrow his clubs surreptitiously, to play on the local municipal links. Father's negative and unhelp-ful attitude made me keener on the game. In due course, I followed his example by trying not to force my tastes upon my sons, so I never encouraged them to take up golf. The result, to my surprise and disappointment, was that they showed little interest in the game. I would have loved it if they had. A possible conclusion is that I should positively have discouraged them from playing, and then, perhaps, they would have developed an enthusiasm.

Golf has been a delight over the years. It has introduced me to countries I might not otherwise have visited, such as Canada, Bermuda, Turkey and Morocco. It has also introduced me to some extraordinary people: Princess Aïsha, the sister of the King of Morocco, the Belgian who invented Godiva Chocolate, Jacques Boursin who invented the eponymous cheese, people of many different backgrounds. If it had not been for the St Germain and Royal Belgium golf clubs, I would certainly never have met so many people nor made so many friends in France and Belgium. Royal Mid-Surrey, my London club, has been a home from home – not only for the golf, but also for the card games and the 'male bonding'. It is a tragedy that the club house has recently burned down; things will never be the same there.

The Law Society Golf Club organises each year, in common with many such professional golfing societies, golf matches against similar associations. It is, how-ever, unique in having so many annual international matches: not only against the Law Societies of Scotland, Ireland and Wales, but also against the Bars and Law Societies of France, Belgium, Holland, Germany, the Channel Islands, Canada and Bermuda. This is because of the tireless efforts of its Honorary Secretary, David Barker, who has devoted his life to the Club. He even organises, every three years, an international tournament, open to teams of lawyers from across the world. No organisation in the world of golf could be better run and nothing in the world of sport has given so much pleasure.

Surprisingly closely linked to golf is another passion, mushrooms. I love wild mushrooms: penny buns, lawyers' wigs or ink caps, bay boletes and chanterelles. In Britain they are largely ignored and considered to be poisonous toadstools. True, there are poisonous ones, but they are few and the rule is simple: only eat what you know. In the autumn, golf courses are full of wild mushrooms and it is rare for me to return home without carrying a delicious supper in my bag. We go on organised mushroom outings once or twice a year with a knowledgeable guide, to learn more about different species. Golf courses remain the main hunting field, but one does have to be careful. One autumn day we went to a fine old golf club near London, called New Zealand. It has nothing, so far as I know, to do with the country of that name. We picked some superb specimens and a man came up to us. I showed him what we had found and he seemed interested. He then told us he was the secretary of the club. He asked us to leave immediately because we were trespassing. I wrote a grovelling letter of apology and we may now return as often as we wish, so long as we let him know that we are coming.

During my convalescence lawn bowls has replaced golf. It is a less energetic but still wonderful game played in the South of England on a large flat grass rink in the summer, and indoors on a carpeted rink in the winter. Everyone dresses in white. Matches are between teams of four, with six matches on a rink, so there can be forty-eight people on the rink at the same time. The co-ordinated movements of the players are a veritable ballet – a beautiful sight. There are some young people who play, but most are old and seem to go on playing well into their eighties or even nineties. I hope that I will be one of them.

CHAPTER 4

You'll never walk alone

When I was two, we moved from a Victorian house in Onslow Road, Fairfield, into a new five-bedroom semi-detached stucco house, 'Killen', named after the Johnston family property in County Tyrone. The address was 56 Childwall Valley Road, Liverpool 16. Childwall is a suburb of Liverpool and, when we moved there, it was on the edge of the country. The maid, Gertie MacArdle, who acted as my nanny, would walk with me to the nearest farm to buy eggs. On our return, we would have tea, toast and a boiled egg – still my favourite food. When I was older, I would go to the farm that delivered the milk and help out – just for the fun of it. The house was fairly standard of its type with one major alteration: the conversion of a large bedroom into a bathroom, always cold because it had a flat roof. The house had no central heating and was heated by coal fires in the kitchen and living room and with gas or electric fires elsewhere. We had a heavy black telephone in the hall. After three minutes conversation the phone would ping, and Father would shout that time was up. As an economy, I was taught to put the light out on leaving the room. This got me into trouble later because people in the office protested when I put out the lights on leaving any room, including the lavatory.

Mother maintained the garden and, like me, she was a hacker. Plants were regimented. I helped by cutting the grass and pruning the roses. When very young, I woke up early one morning and, because I thought it would look nice, cut off all the white flowers from a large bush and arranged them along the fence. I was surprised to discover that Mother was not pleased. There was a slope down from the house to the road, on which Father would park the car. I frightened everyone once by getting into the car and letting off the brake. It shot down the slope and across the road backwards. Luckily there was less traffic in those days and I came to no harm. When rescued, I said, 'I had a lovely ride.' [3]

Killen, Liverpool

Suburban life was livelier then. It certainly looked busier, with more people out of doors. The local shops, within five minutes' walk, included two banks, two paper shops, a fishmonger, two greengrocers, two grocers, a baker, a dairy, a chemist, a hairdresser and an excellent municipal lending library. My mother went shopping most days and indulged in a good chat with the shopkeepers and her neighbours. Milk was delivered early every morning from the local farm by horse and cart. It was in bottles with silver or gold tops depending on quality. Birds pierced the tops and drank the milk from the bottles on the front step. During the war, the girls in the Land Army delivered the milk, dressed in their uniform of wide hats, sweaters and knee breeches. A selection of buses and trams fanned out from the

3   Strangely, Jimmy did the same thing in Brussels. He grabbed the steering wheel; the car turned, and it stopped before reaching a very busy main road.

city centre. There were so few cars that people got angry if anyone parked outside their house. There were hardly any restaurants and no coffee shops except for the Kardomah and Lyons, in the centre of the city. The supermarket had not been invented. There was a lot of bustle and human contact, and a lively pub culture, not that my mother would have dreamed of ever setting foot in a pub.

The Blitz had damaged the city severely. The blight caused by the post-war architects and planners was starting. Most people still lived in small 'slum' houses in bleak looking streets, but they formed warm, friendly and caring neighbour-hoods. Everybody knew each other and front steps were scrubbed white. These communities were being destroyed and their inhabitants were being moved to large impersonal council estates in distant suburbs or into tower blocks. The vibrant heart of the city was torn out and Liverpool, like other British provincial cities, has never recovered.

Siblings

Father made no distinction between the sexes so far as careers were concerned. Indeed he was, I think, a feminist. He insisted that his children have a 'profession'. This was important to him, and a profession did not merely mean going to university – it meant a qualification that would provide a measure of job security. My elder sister Peggy became a doctor. In 1942 this was fairly rare for a woman: in Peggy's year there were three out of about a hundred medical students. She was definitely the apple of my father's eye and he was very proud of her. Joan, my middle sister, was also bright, tall and good looking. She went to Anstey Physical Education College, near Birmingham, and became a PE teacher.

Both my sisters married. Peggy had to wait a year after qualifying, because her fiancé, Ken Oldfield, who was a fellow medical student, failed his final exami-nations. Ken had worked for ICI in their laboratory in Runcorn and ICI had paid for him to go to university. Peggy spent the year obtaining a diploma in obstetrics. I remember her telling horrifying stories about not allowing deformed babies to survive. In some ways it was a tougher world then. When they had both qualified, Father advanced the money to buy a medical practice near Thirsk in the North Riding of Yorkshire. This was, of course, before the National Health Service came into existence and medical practices were still bought and sold. There was not enough work to keep both Ken and Peggy busy, so Ken started giving anaesthetics in the local hospital at Northallerton. He eventually went to London to study, took his fellowship (he was awarded the Nuffield Prize) and became a consultant anaesthetist. Peggy took over the practice and ran it alone. Local farmers and farm workers were shocked at first at having to consult a woman doctor. She told me of one farmer, an exception, who said that he was happier to show her his behind than he was to disclose his financial situation to his accountant. Peggy's practice covered approximately the same area as that of the local vet, Alf Wight. He wrote books under the pseudonym of James Herriot and these are still on the best-seller lists. They were good friends and he sometimes gave his manuscripts to Peggy to read. Peggy would recognise who the characters were in real life, much to Alf's delight.

Ken was a man of original ideas. His views were never what one might expect and this made him good company. Conversation with him was never boring. He was passionate about his hobbies. First came cows; he bought a few and learned everything that there was to be known about them. Then it was horses. Afterwards came birds, and he became a 'twitcher'. After Peggy's early death from cancer in 1972, he became a Roman Catholic and spent a lot of time at Ampleforth Abbey. He also accompanied pilgrimages to Lourdes as a medical adviser. Ken married twice more and his widow, Dorothy, the former county librarian of York, lives near Thirsk. Peggy might have died a little earlier, but she wanted to watch the Wimbledon final. The day of her funeral, people stood three deep along the path to Leake Church. It was the best haymaking day for weeks, but for miles around, the fields were empty. Peggy's death was a shock to me. I knew that she was ill, but the dreaded word cancer was not mentioned. My grief was mixed with anger – there were so many things I wanted to talk to her about and I was not given the opportunity. This is in part why I am so open about my own cancer.[4]

Peggy and Ken had three children, Christopher, Charlotte and Robert. Christopher married Lois, a schoolmate from the local town, Northallerton. He took a degree in biology, edited a related magazine, became a hill farmer and ended up owning an old people's home in Lyme Regis. As he said: 'If you can farm sheep, you can certainly farm people.' Christopher died in 1994 from a brain tumour, but I am in close contact with Lois and her daughters. There are three girls, Kate, Annabel and Lotte. Kate has married Andrew Howard, whose mother is a good friend of Chloë's. One day in the Tube a few years ago, I sensed that a pretty girl sitting opposite was looking at me and was surprised when she followed me on to the platform – I thought that I had made a conquest. She asked if I was Bill Blackburn and said that she was Annabel, my great-niece. Kate and Lotte, when Lotte was still in her early teens, produced three best-selling books: *Nails*, about painting nails, *Body Art*, about decorating the skin, and *Barefaced Chic*, about body painting and temporary tattoos.

Charlotte, Peggy's daughter, married a local Yorkshire estate agent, Harvey Bigg. They have one adopted son, Ashley. Harvey and his father sold their estate agency at the time when it became fashionable for building societies, banks and insurance companies to have an estate agency arm. They retired to Malta on the proceeds and live on the island – spending their time sailing around the Mediterranean.

Ken and Peggy's younger son, Robert, joined the Merchant Marine for a few years. He found the life unsatisfying and went on to art school. He now owns a business that designs and builds exhibitions. He is married to Sue Ker. They live in York and have a son, Tom.

My sister Joan married Tommy Morris, a schoolmaster, who became the

4 I have an 'occult primary' in the head or neck. A lump was removed from the right side of my neck in 1999, followed by radiotherapy. Further lumps appeared on the left side in 2000. All these tumours were secondary. My lymph glands were removed from that side and further radiotherapy followed. In 2001, further secondary tumours reappeared on the right side of my neck. The surgeon, Peter Rhys Evans of the Royal Marsden Hospital, has removed all the remaining lymph glands and my jugular vein. Currently, the news is good – the scans show no remaining tumours. Rhys Evans is famous for his care of John Diamond, the *Times* journalist and the author of *Cowards get Cancer Too*.

headmaster of a school for difficult children in Liverpool. Tommy had an outstanding war record in North Africa, received the Military Medal and was commissioned in the field. My mother was strongly against Joan's relationship with Tommy and did her best to stop the marriage. She was always horrid to Tommy. She hated the fact that he was from a Catholic working class background. Tommy was saint-like in return and always treated my mother with respect and kindness. There was no trace of anti-Catholic feeling in my father, notwithstanding his 'Orange' Protestant background, and he always, most wisely, said that he was not prepared to risk losing a daughter just because she was marrying someone of her own choice. Joan and Tommy have one daughter, Lisa (another Elizabeth), born in 1969, who has an MSc in Educational Psychology and who works in Rotherham. She is married to a maths graduate schoolmaster, Andy (Andrew) Walker. Lisa is a feisty girl with a strong personality. I went to her wedding feeling rather frail, just after an operation. She stopped next to me on her way up the aisle, took me in her arms, and kissed me enthusiastically on the lips saying, 'I want you to be the last man I kiss before I get married.'

CHAPTER 5

You speak French?

In 1947 I was fifteen and went to the World Boy Scout Jamboree near Paris. It was that very hot summer, just after the end of the war. The French were short of wheat so they had asked the American government for 'corn'. Delighted, the US authorities shipped thousands of tons of maize to France. The resulting bread was good when still warm, but as soon as it cooled it became rock hard. Father suggested that I should call on the Savins. In 1938 Peggy had been to stay with them, returning to England at the time of the Munich crisis. She had gone to France on an exchange scheme, organised by one her teachers. The next year one of the Savin daughters was to have come to stay with us. Because of the outbreak of war in 1939, the second half of the exchange never took place. Savin was a Counsellor at the Cour des Comptes (the French National Audit Authority), with a flat near the Bois de Boulogne and a country house near Parthenay in central France. There were two girls in the family, the younger just a little older than me. The elder sister became a doctor, inspired, she said, by Peggy's example. Madame Savin said that she had friends, also at the Cour des Comptes, with a son my age, and that it might be a good idea if we did an exchange. Next year, aged sixteen, I was sent off to the Dordogne to stay with Arnaud de Segogne.

This exchange lasted year after year, with me going to France and Arnaud coming to England. We both profited, I enormously. It certainly had an effect on my appreciation of the good things of life. After my first visit to the Segognes, Peggy, then aged thirty, took me to a restaurant for dinner. We ordered trout. They were served without their heads. I sent them back and called for the chef. I explained that trout should be served with the head, and that the best part of a trout is the flesh of the cheek. Peggy was quite amused by what I had learned in France, but found me an embarrassment.

Arnaud's mother was the daughter of a Toulouse lawyer and had inherited her father's country house, Le Pech, at St André Allas, near Sarlat. Here the family spent their summers and entertained their friends. Arnaud's father, Henry de Segogne, was a charismatic charmer. He transferred from the Cour des Comptes to the State Council, France's highest Administrative Appeals Court. Eventually he became a State Counsellor, a prestigious office, but he never seemed to do any legal work. He was a founder of the elite Groupe de Haute Montagne Section of the French Alpine Club, and had led a French Expedition to the Himalayas. He had also organised the Royal visit to Paris in 1938. He became President of the National Committee for the Preservation of Historic Monuments and travelled widely throughout France, taking notes for a series of guides he was writing. Sometimes he took us with him. We all three camped. He seemed to know everyone. He loved good food and good wine. I learned to drink Château La Tour 1945 and 1947 and to distinguish it from Château Petrus. He was a wonderful man in so many ways, but he was impatient with Arnaud. In fact, both the Segogne parents were judgmental and critical of their children. They made them feel that they were a disappointment. The situation was quite embarrassing, because Henry also made it clear, without exactly saying so, that I was the sort of son he would have liked to have. Luckily, Arnaud was not upset or jealous. He in turn received something from my family for which he is still grateful: uncritical love and affection. Even at the age of fifteen, he was capable of sitting on my mother's knee and just being loved.

Arriving in the Dordogne in midsummer at a fine country house was a revelation to me. I had never experienced anything like it. I can still smell the *tripes à la mode de Caen* simmering for lunch. I can hear the crickets and sense the heat. The terrace, with its fabulous view, was cool and we would sit under the lime trees or walk down to the spring from which water was pumped for the house. Almost all the food was new to me. I would take a little and then, having discovered how good it was, I would pile my plate when offered a second helping. It was sad to discover that salad and cheese are never passed around twice in France.

The Grottes de Lascaux had just been found.[5] The boy who had discovered the caves, while rescuing his dog which had fallen down a hole, showed us round, accompanied by the famous dog. We visited Beynac and Castelnaud, two castles on each side of the Dordogne. There were hardly any tourists then and we camped in the courtyard of Castelnaud. This would be impossible today. Last time I was at Castelnaud there were hordes of visitors: it has become a much-visited museum of mediaeval weaponry. On the terrace in the early morning at Castelnaud, waking up and looking out from our tent, I remember the mist covering the valley below us – it felt as though one could walk on it over the Dordogne river to Beynac. The minor roads were not paved and I recall the plume of white dust streaming out behind the cars. We were invited to lunch by the owners of the nearest chateau, Puymartin. The meal started simply enough, with an egg slowly cooked in olive oil. I had never tasted anything so good. Then came truffles. A butler in full fig served us – another new experience. After lunch, we caught crayfish, placing rotting meat on circular nets, letting them down into the stream and pulling them up again as soon as the crayfish had settled on the meat. They made a delicious supper back at Le Pech.

The local town, Sarlat, was accessible by bicycle. It was then an unspoiled medieval town. Much later it became a tourist centre. Henry de Segogne was instrumental in founding the summer festival, which still takes place, and one of the streets is named after him. From all this, you may gather that Henry de Segogne lived in some style. He was a member of the most exclusive dining club in France, Le Club des Cents, and spent money in restaurants without restraint. Strangely enough his favourite restaurant in Paris was Chez Allard – now the favourite of my son, Alexander. As a State Councillor, he received a civil servant's salary. When he

5   Later, Henry de Segogne became President of the Grottes de Lascaux Society. When I took Pitche to Le Pech, the caves had been closed to the public for years. However, Henry got her in by presenting her as his secretary.

retired, he became a director of a company associated with the Paris Metro, and had a useful expense account. Nevertheless, he died poor, owing money to the French fiscal authorities. Arnaud's sister, Anne, married an architect, Philippe Roque, who died young. One of her daughters, Valentine, is my godchild. Anne has retained Le Pech and spends every summer there.

In the summer of 1949, I was staying at Le Pech. Another guest asked if my father had any money. I said that I thought he did have some. Well, he said, you must call him and tell him that he must not believe Stafford Cripps (the British Chancellor). Tell him my name is René Mayer, that the pound will be devalued by thirty per cent, and that the devaluation will happen within ten days. Although it was not that simple in those days to make international telephone calls, I did as I was told. I did not know that René Mayer was the French Minister of Finance. My father did, and he sold his government stocks and converted them into industrial shares. In this way he lost no money because of the devaluation. Today insider trading is an offence – I wonder whether it was then. My father was so delighted that, from that moment, he encouraged me to go to France whenever I liked. Indeed, as soon as I could drive, he provided me with a van in the summer so that Arnaud and I could go touring and camping on my side of the Channel.

Arnaud and I got on well. We went climbing with the Union Nationale des Centres de Montagne (UNCM) at Les Contamines in the French Alps. There, we lived in pretty primitive conditions, sleeping in dormitories. We were, however, copiously fed and provided with experienced guides, who taught us climbing techniques. We scaled the major peaks around Chamonix, including Mont Blanc, and slept in mountain huts. We started in the very early morning so as to be on the rock faces before they warmed up and before stones began to fall. One year, with Arnaud's Scout Troup, we hiked all around Mont Blanc, crossing to Martigny in Switzerland and continuing through Courmayeur in Italy before ending up back in France at Les Contamines. French Scouts are Catholic and we sang grace before every meal and said prayers every day. We also sang a lot of old French folk songs – I can remember the odd one, and sometimes surprise French people by getting up at legal or golfing dinners and singing *Le Trente-et-un du Mois d'Août* along with the best of them.

On this side of the Channel, Arnaud and I went camping with my Scout Troop. We went climbing in North Wales. We bicycled from Liverpool to see my sister near Thirsk in Yorkshire and then continued, camping, all the way to Edinburgh. It would, I think, be rather too dangerous to do that today, with current traffic conditions. We were heavily laden with our camping gear and it was hard work uphill or against the wind. We rambled in the Lake District and, after my father had given me the use of a van, we drove to the west of Scotland and climbed the Black Cuillins on the Isle of Skye.

Arnaud was religious and tried unsuccessfully to become a priest. Then he tried to join the army and applied to get into St Cyr (the French equivalent of Sandhurst). He did his military service as a paratrooper during the Algerian war and was, I am sure, very brave. Then he went to work for Air France in the reservations department, but ended up with Air Liquide (the French equivalent of British Oxygen) in various capacities. His last job was as manager of the headquarters building in Paris. I introduced him to his wife. One of the secretaries at Theodore Goddard in Paris was a small French girl from an aristocratic family, Gabrielle de Lavenne de Choulot de Chabaud la Tour (sic). She was attractive and sexy. Arnaud did not show a great interest in girls, so I introduced him to Gaby, never thinking that it would lead to anything other than an enjoyable flirtation. I even explained to Arnaud what I had in mind. It turned out differently. Arnaud was of the appropriate background; Gaby fell in love, and married him. The world is small. Anthony Sampson's wife, Sally, used to stay as a young girl with the Choulots and became a friend of Gaby. These days, we see rather more of Anthony and Sally, who live in London, than of Arnaud and Gabrielle, who have retired to the South of France.

Arnaud and Gaby had three children, but lost one in the most appalling circumstances. They were living in Ghana and left the baby in the house with a nurse. The nurse was not attentive and the child managed to overturn and then roll in the contents of a bottle of bleach. Sadly , despite being flown urgently to Europe for treatment the burns were such that the baby died *en route*. Arnaud, in retirement, remains much involved with Opus Dei, the Roman Catholic sect, and goes to Mass every day. There are two surviving daughters, whom I hardly know. Armelle, also a follower of Opus Dei, is married and has many children. Anne-Louise is an actress, and apparently a very good one.

CHAPTER 6

Wine and sex

Father sent me off to University with good advice. He called me in to see him, rather formally, and said that he had two things to say to me, one very serious and one less so. I asked him to tell me the very serious thing first. 'Never order a half bottle of wine,' he said. 'Even when you are on your own, you will find that it is not quite enough.' 'Well, what else, then?' I asked. 'Don't have anything to do with homosexuality,' he said, straight-faced. 'It is dirty and disappointing.' Other advice that I remember was about tying a bow tie. I did it three or four times until it was to his satisfaction. Father then switched off the light and made me tie it in the dark. I asked him why. 'You'll find out when you're older,' he said.

Not at all *à propos*, I joined the University Air Squadron, flying Chipmunks and Harvards in my spare time, and became an Acting Pilot Officer. The Squadron Leader called us together and announced that the Air Ministry had decreed that we needed to have five Acting Pilot Officers, to be chosen by examination. He announced the names of the five members of the Squadron whom he thought deserved promotion. He then asked us whether we agreed with his choice. Nobody dared express a contrary opinion. We all sat the examination, but we chosen five were given an hour to study the questions, and the answers. The Squadron provided a great social life. We were paid to fly and could run up mess bills; there were many parties and dances.

My childhood sweetheart Pam Milnes and I became engaged. She was the daughter of the chemistry master at my school. I had the use of Father's car, which I drove dangerously and sometimes drunkenly. I managed to get a law degree without ever looking up a single law case. It was only a third class honours degree, but more than I deserved. I cannot remember ever doing any academic work except to swot for examinations and normally scored fifty per cent for accurate reproduction of lecturers' circulated notes, in the complete absence of any original research.

Pop culture had not yet arrived. The Cavern had not yet opened and the Beatles were, presumably, still at Quarry Bank School. We danced to the Blue Tango and to the Ink Spots in the University Students' Union, in the Air Squadron Mess and at parties. The best parties were at the local hospitals, with the medical students and their nurse girlfriends. We went to pubs and, when they closed, we moved on to shebeens, the illegal drinking clubs in private houses that stayed open all night. They were patronised mainly by policemen, prostitutes and criminals. They all tolerated the university students or 'college boys' as we were known. We were quite safe, and the drinkers would move to protect us immediately if trouble broke out, as it often did.

Without effort or much thought, I slipped into articles of clerkship with a small local Liverpool law firm and qualified as a solicitor. I then had a bad accident on a motorcycle while returning from a training flight and spent many weeks in hospital. I had hitched a lift, riding pillion, from the airfield to the officers' mess. We crossed a main road and hit the side of a van. The driver of the motorcycle broke his back and I, behind him, without a helmet, ended up with a scarred and fractured skull, an open fracture of the left leg and a broken left arm and elbow. The police came to my parents' house and said that, if they wanted to see me alive, they must go immediately to Walton Hospital. They rushed them and my sister Joan to the hospital in the police car at full speed. The surgeon was proposing to amputate my leg, but a young Australian doctor said that I was too young. He persuaded the surgeon to set it and, although it is not a pretty sight, it works well. The RAF awarded a war disability pension of forty per cent, which I still receive. In January 2000, the War Pensions authority sent a doctor to examine me, and he confirmed the forty per cent. In my working life I used the pension to buy clothes. Father had always said, 'If you work for yourself, your appearance does not matter, but, if you work for someone else, you need a good suit and a good fountain pen.'

At the end of the University law course, when I needed to go to Law School, Father became ill again. I had to oversee his business while he was in hospital and convalescent. Consequently I had to delay taking Solicitors' Finals. Not wanting to

Pilot officer

get married until fully qualified, I explained to my childhood sweetheart Pam the necessity of postponing our wedding. To my surprise, Pam's reaction was one of fury. She would brook no delay. She said that the consultation was merely to inform her of a *fait accompli* and that this was a decision I could not take on my own. Clearly in her home the women took the decisions. I decided that, if I wanted to remain master of my life, it would be better to withdraw from the engagement. This I did, and she did not return the engagement ring. Pam married a mutual friend, Peter Swinnerton, and I never saw her again. I was truly in love with her. My hand trembled and my heart thumped, not only in her presence, but even when I thought about her. However, looking back, I think that the marriage would have been a disaster. We were both stubborn, used to getting our own way and very immature.

CHAPTER 7

Which firm did you train with?

Free from any sentimental or other attachment, the prospect of a career in the local Liverpool firm of solicitors to which I had been articled did not inspire. I had not forgotten the advice of Henry de Segogne: that the law was a fine career and the future lay in the international field. I heard of a job with the major London firm Theodore Goddard & Co,[6] was interviewed and accepted. I moved to France immediately and started work in the Paris office. Arnaud was away in Algeria doing military service and the Segognes welcomed me as their English son, installing me in their flat near the Trocadero in Arnaud's room, actually a maid's room in the attic of the building.

So in 1957 I started work as an assistant in the Paris office of Theodore Goddard. At that time it was the only London law firm in Paris. The offices were in the rue St Honoré on the corner of the rue Cambon and we shared them with an American lawyer, Sam Mercer, who lived above. Derek Wise was the boss and we had a couple of secretaries. Derek Wise became the doyen of English lawyers in Paris. He was legal adviser to the British Ambassador and was awarded the CBE for his services to the British Government.

I was paid little at the beginning, and lived to some extent on the generous free food and lodging of the Segognes. The office was not very profitable and was

6 Now called just Theodore Goddard.

run on a cash basis, so nothing could be spent until the fees had been paid and the money received.[7] Luckily, my father had given me £1,000 (the equivalent today of over £16,000) on my twenty-first birthday to compensate for the fact that my sisters had each received a legacy of £500 from his brother William Howard on their twenty-first birthdays. This money, used bit by bit, enabled me to live fairly well. When my son Alexander became twenty-one, I gave him £1,000 for having refrained from smoking,[8] so the tradition continued. Perhaps my sons will give £1,000 to their sons when they become twenty-one – but by then it will be a disappointingly small amount.

The work was varied and fascinating. We had big corporate clients such as British Rail, but also a lot of personal work, some of it for rich and famous clients such as King Farouk, the Patinos and the Clores. I handled divorces and traffic accident claims, formed companies, and recovered debts. In fact, I invented an effective method of debt collection. While winding up the former dress houses of Paquin and Worth, I found that a number of aristocratic French ladies had never settled their dress bills. Letters did not seem to have any effect until I wrote to them saying that, if they did not settle their accounts, all future correspondence would be by postcard. They paid up immediately, presumably because they did not want their concierges, or maybe their husbands, to know these intimate details of their lives.

I remember one young woman who had married a Frenchman. She came to see us when the marriage was on the rocks. This was hardly surprising since she spoke virtually no French and he spoke not a word of English. She had decided to go back to America and asked if she could leave a few things, so that her husband could not sell them. I put a picture on the wall behind my desk. I asked her whether I could use the car, a beautiful Lancia Grand Turismo, and she agreed. How I enjoyed that car, my only sports car ever. The small strongbox went into the office safe

---

7   Later we changed the accounting system to a 'work in hand and bills delivered' system. This meant that the value of current work, and the amount of bills delivered but not yet paid, could be included in the calculation of profit.

8   Jimmy had the same offer as Alexander, but exercised the option to smoke.

unopened. We thought that we had better insure the painting and were amazed at its value. It was a large Miró. She never returned and asked us to dispose of the items. To avoid any dispute, we opened the strongbox in the presence of a Court Bailiff; it contained a piece of string and a conker, nothing else.

The firm had a reputation for matrimonial work dating back to Mrs Simpson and Edward VIII. I handled a few divorces. One client was a model at Dior. After the proceedings were over, she rang and invited me to lunch, asking whether I would mind if some photographs were taken of us during the meal. I had no objection and we met on the terrace of Chez Francis, an excellent restaurant in the Place de l'Alma. The photographer was not intrusive. I never saw the resulting publicity (for Colman's Mustard) but the senior partner in London did. He telephoned me to explain that being a male model was not compatible with the status of a Theodore Goddard partner.

The firm's clients included people the like of whom I had never even dreamed existed. A new world opened up of rich and powerful people, many of whom had enormous egos and were frightful snobs. The beautiful Diana Cooper, for example, was not alone in treating me as a servant. At lunch in the Ritz, Lord Tredegar, the descendant of Henry Morgan the pirate and heir to the South Wales coalfields, kept saying 'fuck' in mixed company. I was shocked and it must have shown. He explained that this was because I was a bourgeois and that aristocrats of his ilk, in common with the working class, used bad language.

Lady Kenmare, heir to the Cunard shipping line millions, received in her bath at her villa on the Pointe St Hospice du Cap Ferrat. She had five villas on the Pointe and was angry that the local tax inspector had dared to impose taxes on the income from her lettings. The income was calculated in such a way that the tax was under £1,000 per year but this type of client did not think that laws applied to them. For her it became a matter of principle and she threatened to leave the country. The charming tax inspector explained that he was under pressure from his superiors in Paris and we compromised for an even smaller amount of tax. There was at this time strict, but largely ineffective, exchange control regulation. One client bought a nice flat in Paris, with Bank of England consent. She decided she did not like it and, before disposing of it, bought another. I rang her influential banker son (it was all sorted out on the international banking old boys' net) and was asked to go to a French bank to pick up the purchase price of the second flat – in cash. Another client returned regularly from Africa with a suitcase of French Colonial francs. I would take it round to a French Bank which nowadays is a household name for respectability. Next day, his account in Switzerland would be credited with Swiss francs at a rate of exchange favourable to the bank.

Karim, the Aga Khan, was a client. He thought that a French newspaper had libelled him and he wanted to sue for damages. We explained that the amount of damages awarded in France would be small in comparison to England. However, he also took the matter as being one of principle. We took him to see Maître Floriot, the most famous French *avocat* of his generation, who received us at his high desk, posed upon a lion skin. We sat in low chairs looking up to him, the great lawyer. Karim leaned back, crossed his legs and placed them carefully on the head of the lion. We did sue and came to a settlement, preparing a highly flattering article which the newspaper was happy to print.

We acted for BOAC, the long-distance predecessor of British Airways. It was opening up the route to South America and the planes needed to refuel and to slip crews at Dakar on the way there and back. The legal staff of BOAC did not speak or write French, so they asked us to negotiate for permanent rooms in a hotel, landing rights and a shop in Dakar. There were no hotel rooms so we paid for the owner to build a new floor at our expense. When I had finished and the bill was paid, the airline offered a return ticket to Dakar. It seemed further and more exotic in those days. I made good use of introductions from French friends and was treated with great courtesy by the hotel owner, whose fortune I may have made.

We also acted for Marks & Spencer before they had opened stores in Paris and the main French provincial cities. We formed a company to protect the name. In those days the President of a French company had to be French, so Pitche stepped in. Wearing her best hat and dress for the occasion, she attended the beginning of every board meeting so that her presence could be noted. One day we received a call from the Legal Director of Marks & Spencer in London. He explained that Jonathan, the son of the Chairman, Lord Sieff, was going to marry a French girl, in Paris, and asked whether we would help get the necessary papers. I was detailed to do the job. A short time before the wedding, I received a panic call: the bride had turned out to be Monegasque and not French. As a foreigner, she needed the same papers as Jonathan and nothing had been done. Time was short. Could I drop everything and take the company Rolls, the chauffeur and the girl, to do what was necessary? The papers were ready on time and, to my surprise, I received an invitation to the wedding reception. This took the form of a lunch in the private rooms of the Tour d'Argent. When I arrived (and it was the first time I had been in a three star restaurant), I expected to be seated well below the salt. Not at all: I was ushered to the right hand of Lord Sieff who, during his speech, said that the wedding could never have taken place without my help.[9]

Looking back, I was no great lawyer – merely an efficient practitioner. However, I liked the work and earned my nickname of 'Room at the Top Bill' through ambition and energy. Perhaps my lasting contribution to the office was to invent and introduce an efficient filing system. It was still in use until Theodore Goddard, Paris, merged with a French law firm some years ago.

Theodore Goddard remains a leading London law firm. It is named after a lawyer who had retired shortly before I joined. As I have said, he had made his reputation by acting for Mrs Simpson in her divorce and subsequent marriage to the Duke of Windsor. Major clients of the firm included press barons and their newspapers and I got to know the Carr family, the owners of the *News of the World*, who often came to Paris. The firm acted for Profumo in the notorious case. (While a Government Minister in office, he slept with Christine Keeler who was sleeping at the same time with the Russian Naval Attaché.) I took delight in reading the file when in London.

9   The private rooms of the Tour d'Argent have become a favourite place for celebrations. We used them both for Alexander's civil wedding lunch and for Chloë's seventieth birthday party.

Legal luminaries

The firm was unusual for those days in having women partners. Blanche Lucas was the strongest personality. She was a tall and strikingly beautiful woman of Hungarian Jewish extraction, brought up in Menton, who spoke perfect French, English, German, and Hungarian. She handled divorce work, always acting for the wives. She danced perfectly and we went dancing a lot when she came to Paris. She was married several times and had many lovers – but she confessed that she found it impossible to spend a whole night with a man. Quite how this qualified her to become the Chair of the Marriage Guidance Council remains a mystery to me. She was also the President of the Solicitors' European Group. At one of its meetings, the platform was composed of the great and the good of the profession. She leaned across and whispered, 'It is difficult for me to take those men seriously. I have seen most of them with their trousers around their ankles.' She died of cancer, still entertaining the nurses with her unusual views on men and on marriage. At her request, we left the church at the end of her memorial service dancing down the aisle to the strains of the *Continental*.

The senior partner was John Brooks, who became notorious as the 'Spanking Colonel'. He was the youngest Colonel in the British army when taken prisoner in Singapore by the Japanese. He spent the war in Changi prison camp and this experience must have affected his sexual predilections. He came to Paris fairly often and drew out large sums in cash. We soon found out why. One day he borrowed the senior Paris partner's secretary, Janet, to act as his interpreter. She came back looking disturbed. Derek Wise told me to take her for a drink to find out what had happened. She was reluctant to say, but I eventually discovered that she had found herself in a sleazy bar, arranging John Brooks's evening entertainment. He wanted dinner served by three girls, one black, one yellow and one brown, to be whipped afterwards. Apparently, the negotiation about the cost per lash was tough. Some years later, John Brooks sued a newspaper in England for libel. It had published an article saying that he took girls on his boat on the Thames and spanked them. He was awarded a symbolic farthing in damages and was known forever afterwards as the 'Spanking Colonel'. Theodore Goddard lived all this down and is successful and respected.

Derek Wise was a super boss and we have remained good friends. He treated us all very well. As an example of his style, I remember one day I went to lunch with a charming Swedish girl. At the end of the meal, in direct Scandinavian manner, she suggested that we retired somewhere to be alone. The idea excited me, of course, but I remembered that I had an appointment with Derek and a client. I hurried back in rather a bad temper. I must have shown my mood because, when the client had gone, Derek wormed out of me what had happened. He was furious and made me promise that if I received such an offer again I would ring him immediately and he would handle the client on his own. Sadly, I was never able to take up Derek's offer. The occasion never arose.

Every week, the other young English lawyer in Paris, David Goodchild, and I would go for a drink at Pam Pams, a bar in the Champs Elysées. David eventually became a senior partner in Clifford Chance and played a major role in that firm's global expansion. It is now the largest law firm in the world. One evening, he bet the price of the drinks that I could not pick up a girl who was sitting up at the bar drinking Guinness. She turned out to be from Bolton, working as a Bluebell dancer at the Lido. Our relationship was difficult, because I worked from 9am until about 7pm, and she worked from 10pm until 3am. I could see her for an hour or so after the office or I could leave the office, go to bed, get up at 3am and then meet her. After some weeks of this latter regime, Derek said that I was looking rather tired and should consider changing my life-style. That was the end of that.

Parisian integration

When Arnaud returned from Algeria, I moved in with a new friend, Jacques Seydoux. His father was the French Ambassador to Austria and we were able to live in his family flat in Paris. The Seydoux are an old French Protestant family. As such, Jacques was a member of the Haute Société Protestante or 'HSP'. He was invited out a lot to smart parties and I tagged along. It was understood, he told me, that he must, in due course, marry a Protestant girl, preferably from a banking family. Henry de Segogne insisted that I took French lessons from his old French teacher at the Lycée Henri IV, so my French moved from being fast and approximate to being good and accurate. This really helped my social life. Arnaud's friends also adopted me. They were Catholic and very well behaved. They described themselves as the 'BIMCD', standing for 'Beautiful, Intelligent, Modest, Chaste and Desirable'. I think that I was perhaps the least chaste. After a year or so, I became a local partner in the firm and two more lawyers joined us. I began to earn enough to live on, albeit modestly, and even bought a little car, a Renault Dauphine.

Bill Blackburn had always seemed a decent enough name, but I discovered that it did not sound as good in French as in English. It took me some time to find out that I had an unflattering nickname. Apparently *les burns* in old French slang means testicles and I learned that I was known as 'Couilles noires' alias 'Blackballs'. Indeed, when I went with a client to see a French *avocat*, he greeted us with laughter, saying how pleased he was to meet 'Couilles noires' at last. Luckily the client's French was not good enough for him to understand and I did not bother to explain the exchange.

CHAPTER 8

What is going to become of us?

After a couple of years in Paris, I was settling in and enjoying life. One evening I went for a couscous supper to a friend's, Tanguy Lefebvre-Dibon. I sat on the floor next to a small, delicate, blonde and blue-eyed French girl, who spoke perfect English. I particularly noticed her fine ankles and wrists. She had been to a Catholic convent school, Les Oiseaux, at Margate. Her parents had recently returned from Rome, where her father had been the French Military Attaché. Her name was Marie-Thérèse Dorange, and she was known as 'Pitche'. She had a younger sister, Hélène, so called because she had been born in Athens, and her nickname was 'Koukla', meaning little doll in Greek. Apparently all children in Greece have nicknames because it is considered bad luck to call a child by its real name before it is baptised.

I was told that Tanguy was very attracted to Pitche and as I had met her in his flat it was difficult for me to contact her. At last I plucked up courage and rang Tanguy, making it difficult for him to refuse to allow me to call her. I asked her to lunch and then to dinner. We went out a lot, until one night we went to a restaurant, the Sabretache, near Versailles. This was before the era of credit cards and I was running out of cash. I realised during dinner that I did not have enough money to pay the bill. Then, over coffee and in the gentle candlelight, Pitche said in French, 'What is going to become of us?' To my surprise I heard myself say, 'Why, we are going to get married, of course.' Later I learned that Pitche had been advised to pose that particular question by one of her mother's friends. We passed the tip on to girlfriends wanting to get married, and it worked – not that the marriages were always successful. To return to the restaurant, when the bill came I had to leave my watch as security for future payment. We met in the autumn of 1959 and were married in May 1960. I was twenty-seven and Pitche was twenty-six. Pitche's mother was suspicious of this young Englishman and checked up to see whether I would make an appropriate husband. She went to see Madame Savin and Madame de Segogne. Both, thank goodness, said that they would be delighted to have me as a son-in-law. I went to see Pitche's father. He gave his permission and apologised for having no money. Incidentally, Pitche had been engaged previously to a young banker, Jean-Vincent de St Phalle.

Pitche had been to school in England and to university in Germany. She worked as an assistant to one of her parent's friends, Louis (Loulou) de Fouquières, a retired colonel in the French Air Force, who owned and edited an aircraft magazine. She had also been a hostess in the Vatican Pavilion at the World Fair in Brussels. After our marriage, she continued to work for Loulou and would occasionally go to the UN Food and Agricultural Organisation in Rome (the FAO) to work as a translator at conferences. On one such trip I accompanied her and we went to an extra-ordinary restaurant called Les Eaux Vives run by an order of Belgian nuns to raise money for missionary work. Pitche chatted to the Mother Superior who greeted us, indicating that she would perhaps be tempted to join the Order one day. She was nonplussed by the forceful response. There could be no question of it as the Order only accepted virgins.

My father became very ill and I went to see him just before he died. When he went into the operating theatre he said that he was not going to recover. I was able to tell him that I was hoping to marry a girl called Marie-Thérèse Dorange. He asked if I meant d'Orange-Nassau. When my father died I cried. Then I felt awful having to ask my mother for money to buy an engagement ring – explaining that French girls expected more expensive rings than did English girls. I went with my mother to Wartski's, the Grafton Street jewellers, who had their first shop in Llandudno. My mother said that Wartski would travel around North Wales with a pack on his back, hawking jewellery. We bought a fine diamond and emerald ring, now worn by Kathy, Jimmy's Peruvian wife.

With mother and Pitche

Pitche and I were married on 29 April 1960 at a small civil ceremony in the Town Hall of the 7th Arrondissement in Paris. My boss, Derek Wise, was a witness. We lunched after the ceremony at my father-in-law's club, the Nouveau Cercle. A large turbot was served in its dish – enough for the fourteen people present. A week later, the religious ceremony took place at Pitche's grandmother's home at Belloy sur Mer in the Somme. In French terms, the religious wedding was a small one – about 250 guests. I shocked everyone by disappearing to play golf the day before the ceremony. Quite a lot of my family came, and Arnaud de Segogne was my best man. Pitche and I had photographs taken with our old boyfriends and girlfriends grouped behind us.

The biggest surprise at the wedding was the arrival of two English Roman Catholic priests. They were the sons of my father's nanny, Lizzie Deegan. She had married a merchant seaman and had three sons, who all became priests. Her husband was drowned in the 1939–45 war and my father supported her financially. When the priests heard that I was getting married, they were very pleased because I was marrying a Catholic – all future Blackburns in my line would be Catholic. One of the priests, Dom Maurus, was of the White Benedictine order. This is a closed order that converted from Anglicanism at the beginning of the century. He obtained special permission to come to our wedding – a rare outing for him. When our sons were born, Dom Maurus wrote to remind us that we had undertaken to educate the children in the Catholic faith. He made the arrangements for them to be able to go to Ampleforth – a Benedictine boarding school. A French priest, Jean Charles Roux, married us. He had been a diplomat and a colleague of Pitche's father in Athens. It was the first wedding at which Charles Roux had officiated. Pitche said that he tried hard to persuade her not to go through with it. Happily he failed, and all proceeded according to plan.[10]

---

10   Jean Charles Roux also, on my introduction, officiated at the wedding of Oriana, Chloë's daughter. He gave such an outrageously fundamentalist Catholic homily that most of the congregation were in a state of shock and Oliver, Chloë's son, walked out of the church. This was not one of my more successful recommendations and I am not sure, even now, that I have been forgiven.

The wedding ceremony was held in the family chapel in the grounds of the house. The local bishop created difficulties because I was a Protestant. He refused to allow the bells to be rung, he refused to allow my ring to be blessed and he refused to allow the marriage to be celebrated at the main altar – fortunately there was only one altar in the little chapel. We left before the end of the reception in the English manner, rather than staying to the end in the French way, and drove to Paris. We took the night sleeper to Barcelona, in a wagon-lit with two inter-communicating cabins. We spent the first night in Barcelona in the Ritz, the best hotel in town, hired a car and drove up the Costa Brava. On our return to Barcelona, I had to pay for the car rental and found that I had hardly a peseta left, so we ended up spending our last night in Spain in a fleapit.

The French family

Pitche's father, André, was a cavalry officer in the regular army. He was from a Breton family and Dorange, the family house, is outside the town of Vieux-Vy-sur-Couesnon, near Rennes. The Couesnon is the river that marks the frontier between Brittany and Normandy. It meets the sea at the Mont St Michel and, because it enters the sea to the west of it, it is said to render it Norman rather than Breton. There is English blood in the Dorange family. André's great-grandfather, Magloire Dorange, was an *avocat* from Rennes and he met an English girl, Helen Wilson, in a coach when she was travelling to Paris from Brittany with her mother. She was the daughter of a wholesale tea merchant in the City of London and they married in London, after she had converted to Catholicism. Her mother, also Helen Wilson, eventually became a Catholic and went to live with her daughter in Brittany. She was a great traveller and in 1870 at the age of sixty went on one of the first Cook's package tours to Egypt and the Holy Land. I have transcribed her diary and circulated the text to interested members of the family.

André had spent the war in Algeria and Morocco and was Marshal Juin's *Chef de Cabinet*. As such, he was much involved in the negotiations concerning the landings by US and British troops in North Africa in 1942. His name appears in the chronicles of the period as having played a key role in the arrangements for a cease-fire. General de Gaulle gave him the command of a tank regiment with which he landed at Cavalaire, near Le Canadel. He was wounded in the Rhône Valley and rushed to an American dressing station. He had burnt eyes, but his sight was saved because the US medics had penicillin, then a new drug. He commanded a regiment (the French 2nd Dragoons) in Germany, was the Army's liaison officer with the French Senate, became French Military Attaché in Greece and retired with the rank of full Colonel, having been Military Attaché in Rome. In retirement, he was given the honorary rank of Brigadier General. He was awarded many decorations, including Commander of the Legion of Honour. These can be seen in a frame under glass at Cap Horn, in St Valéry sur Somme. He loved uniforms and was a handsome man. There is an excellent photograph of him in the full dress uniform of the Knights of Malta, posing with Princess Grace of Monaco.

Pitche's mother, Simone, was a beauty, and is still a fine looking woman. She has the most perfect taste in clothes and interior decoration. She is at ease in social situations, and André was proud of her abilities as a hostess. She comes from an industrial family in the Vimeu near Abbeville. The family was presided over by Simone's mother, Cécile Laperche, who owned the Château de Belloy, at Friville-Escarbotin in Picardy, where we got married. It had been a three-storey Victorian horror, but it burned down in the 1950s and was rebuilt with a dormer-windowed first floor and one of the original two towers. In its restored version it became a handsome, old-brick, manor house. It looked good, but the quality of the rebuilding was typical of the time. The partitions and doors were thin and one could hear noises from one end of the bedroom floor to the other. There was a lovely walled kitchen garden and a large wood where the trees had been untouched for many years. They were full of bullets, from the fighting between the British and Germans in 1940. By the time I met her Cécile was a widow. Her husband, Paul Laperche, spoke German and had been the official interpreter for Marshal Foch during the 1914–1918 war. He translated the armistice in the railway carriage in the clearing at Compiègne in 1918 and Simone has a photograph of him, standing on the steps of the carriage.

Cécile lived well on the revenues from the nearby, family-owned, locks and bolts factory, Laperche, which employed about 250 people. She kept open house for all her family. My parents-in-law, André and Simone, together with Odette and Jean Wallut, Simone's sister and brother-in-law, spent a lot of time at Belloy, which is in comparatively easy reach of Paris. Even in those days, before motorways, the drive was well under three hours. My parents-in-law, on their return from Rome, had bought a house called Santa Helena at Le Canadel, near the Lavandou. Holidays not spent at Belloy were spent in Le Canadel. I had no idea that such a lovely place existed until after I had married Pitche. I called it the 'southern bonus'.

Perhaps I should explain the family situation in a little more detail. Simone's father, Paul Laperche, and her brother Jean, were killed in a motor accident. Consequently there was talk of André taking over the running of the locks and bolts business, and retiring from the army. In the end, however, it was Jean's widow, Axelle, who took it on. She made it a condition that she should have control of the majority of the shares. Thus Simone sold her shares to Axelle. With the proceeds, André and Simone bought the Villa Santa Helena. When I married Pitche, I found that my parents-in-law and Pitche thought that the shares had been sold to Axelle too cheaply. My new nuclear family had a complex about being poor in comparison with the extended family. This is the enduring state of affairs in Simone's mind.

Axelle is a strong woman and she ran the family business energetically and successfully. She always saw to it that her mother-in-law had enough money to live well, with all the domestic help necessary to entertain the family and friends. Axelle had arrived in that part of the world as a social worker. She is the daughter of a postman from the Gers Department and still has a slight accent of the Midi. She was good looking with nice legs and caught the eye of Jean, the local rich boy, who married her. Later, after Jean's death, Axelle married Jacques de Crozals, another factory owner. Today, she lives in some state in a beautiful house known as Le Castel, within the walls of the mediaeval castle that dominates St Valéry sur Somme. Simone's sister, Odette, married Jean Wallut, a Parisian stockbroker, the scion of a family of Paris notaries. He had inherited a fortune in Paris real estate, including one side of the rue Scribe, opposite the Grand Hotel, and a part of the adjoining rue Auber. They had five children: Jean-Jacques, Christian, Patrick, Catherine and Sophie.

Family life

Pitche and I set up home in a flat at 19 Avenue de la Motte Picquet in the 7th Arrondissement, near the Ecole Militaire, on the same floor as my parents-in-law, luckily with a separate entrance. I discovered that I had married a wonderful girl, but a less attractive family. André shouted at his wife and Simone screamed back. It was the first time that I had been close to people who were so ill mannered to each other. Koukla, Pitche's younger sister, played each parent off against the other in order to do exactly as she pleased. The parents came to Pitche in turn, each complaining of the behaviour of the other. Pitche remained calm and reasonable and tried her best to smooth things over. It was, however, a great strain for her and the atmosphere created by my parents-in law was disagreeable. We had a Spanish maid, Victoria, who cleaned and cooked. Indeed, Pitche only knew one dish – escalope of veal with rice mixed with green peas. Pitche and I nevertheless settled down well together and were very happy.

I discovered, over time, that I had married an exceptional person. Pitche was intelligent, sensitive, organised and receptive to other people's problems. She was a good listener. When I came home we would share our day's activities. She was the best career adviser I could ever have hoped for; we had a life of true marital complicity. She was a good mother to Alexander and Jimmy, and very authoritative in her quiet way. She was not physically strong and when she took up golf, even if we only played nine holes, she needed to go to bed to rest after the game. However, she had tremendous willpower and even took up jogging at one point. She had bad migraines and she got upset about things. She took everything on her shoulders and suffered accordingly. Her relations with her family sometimes drained her physically and emotionally.

Pitche's grandmother, Cécile, was eager to become a great-grandmother. She would telephone several times a week to ask whether Pitche had become pregnant. She once said at table, 'Is it my fault if I've married an infertile granddaughter to an impotent Englishman?' The babies were slow in coming, but tests showed that I, at least, was *hyper-fertile*. Pitche had a miscarriage on one of her trips to Rome. It was three years before Alexander arrived, followed two years later by Jimmy. They were both beautiful and healthy children.

We had plenty of friends and Pitche's family was large and dominating. Both her parents and her grandmother demanded attention and consideration as of right, but did little to deserve it. Pitche's father, however, turned out to be a wonderful grandfather. He liked photographing the children with his old Leica. He would

Pitche surrounded by her family on the steps at Belloy.
From left to right: André Dorange, Jimmy, Odette Wallut, Camille Bonnier, Jean Wallut, Pitche, myself,
Simone Dorange, Guillaume Bonnier, Alexander, Koukla and Bertrand Bonnier.

play with them for hours and, when they were older, he was of considerable help to them, working hard at vacation tasks and projects.

Koukla, Pitche's sister, had married a young French architect, Bertrand Bonnier. They had two children, Guillaume and Camille, and they lived in the rent-controlled flat at 1 rue Clovis of which I was the official tenant. Alexander and Cari occupy it today. Pitche and I had exchanged our first flat for a larger flat in the rue d'Assas to which the owner wanted to return, and offered the rue Clovis in exchange. We accepted, but never actually lived in the rue Clovis because we went to London. Later, I was able to help Bertrand's career as an architect by introducing him to my colleagues at IBM France and IBM Europe. He designed an education centre for IBM France and the interior of the new IBM Europe headquarters at La Défense near Paris. Sadly, the marriage ended in divorce. Koukla then married Christopher MacLehose, a publisher who led the management buy-out of The Harvill Press from HarperCollins. Christopher is greatly admired as the purist of English publishing. His literary standards are high. His first question to me was, 'Who do you think is the greatest living writer?' I gulped and replied, 'Patrick O'Brian.' To my immense surprise he said that he entirely agreed. They live in London and have two sons, Timothy and Leo.

Koukla has had a successful career in publishing in her own right and is as well known as Christopher in the sector. She worked in Paris for Flamarion and is a literary scout in London, representing a number of well-known continental publishing houses. She is a true support to both my sons, replacing their mother so far as she is able. Ever-present when needed, she has a strong sense of family solidarity. For me, however, she will always be the naughty and self-willed little sister. I remember being on holiday at Le Canadel. Naked on my bed in the heat taking a siesta, I heard the patter of Koukla's feet. She, then about thirteen years old, entered the room and stood at the end of the bed. 'You're much better looking with your clothes on,' she said, and left.

*

Club life

Henry de Segogne made me a member of the Automobile Club on the Place de la Concorde. It is much more exclusive than the English RAC. Before the interview, he made me promise not to reveal that my father had anything to do with the grocery business. Pitche thought that too many members were mere professionals: lawyers, stockbrokers and bankers. She preferred her father's club, the Nouveau Cercle, traditionally the club for country gentlemen. Every month, I went to a dinner held by the Association of Foreign Lawyers. The secretary was a lawyer called Yturbe and the dinner was always in the Jockey Club, the smartest in Paris. The Jockey Club has jurisdiction over the flat racing in France and the Nouveau Cercle over the steeple chasing. At one dinner, Yturbe announced that there would be no dinner the following month because the Jockey Club was closing for refurbishment. I said that I could organise a dinner at the Nouveau Cercle. Through my father-in-law, I did so and it was a success. Back in the Jockey Club the following month, I was congratulated on the food served by 'my' club. It seemed too complicated to explain that it was not my club, but my father-in-law's, and that my club was the Auto, so I just nodded. On my return home I told Pitche what had happened and she said the simplest thing to do was to add the Nouveau Cercle to my club memberships. My father-in-law proposed me and I had to appear in the club, in morning dress, at six o'clock in the evening, so that I could be recognised as a new member.

Some years later the Nouveau Cercle moved in with the Interallié, almost next door to the Auto. I found myself with two clubs, both with swimming pools and gyms. I told Pitche that I was resigning from the Nouveau Cercle. She was furious and forced me to remain a member of the Nouveau Cercle, the more socially prestigious. To complete a long digression about clubs, Alexander eventually took over my membership of the Nouveau Cercle. Then, a few years ago when it closed for refurbishment, its members were given the right to use the facilities of the Auto. When he went there to swim, an old attendant said, 'Ah, your name is Blackburn. We used to have a member of that name, and I still have his shaving bowl and brush.'

CHAPTER 9

Technology buff

Michel Debrabant, who later changed his name to Michel de Brabant, was a good friend of Pitche's. Indeed, he became Jimmy's godfather. One day in 1962, he said that he had seen a job advertised that might suit. It was for a lawyer in the legal department of IBM's European HQ in Paris. One of more than ninety applicants, I got the job. The secretary of the company had died, and the American legal counsel had inherited all the files relating to the company. As he did not speak much French, he was somewhat embarrassed. I was hired as a staff attorney. The new job more than doubled my earnings. IBM was not yet quite the phenomenal success it was to become, but it was extremely prosperous and had a virtual monopoly of the data processing market. This was the time when technology was moving from Hollerith punch card machines to computers. I was being given the opportunity to become associated with the world's greatest technological success, the growth of the computer market.

Life at IBM was enjoyable, as well as being stimulating and exciting. Our offices were in the Cité du Retiro off the Faubourg St Honoré, just behind Hermès. They were well appointed. Rumour had it that one of the older buildings on the site had been a well-known Parisian brothel known as the Sphinx and it was said that one could see the marks of bidets under the carpets of the offices. My job was to handle all the problems of the small French Headquarters Company, employing about 500 people. I did all the local legal work, sometimes with the help of colleagues in the legal department of IBM France. This involved board and other corporate formalities, plus real estate and personnel matters. The majority of the senior employees were on assignment from abroad, so I worked a lot on their employment contracts and work permits. It was not always easy to obtain work permits for American employees but we had a couple of former police inspectors on the books who eased the passage through the French bureaucratic jungle.

The headquarters of IBM France, containing the legal department of the French operating company, were not far away, in the Place Vendôme. I discovered that the IBM France building was in fact owned by IBM Europe and leased to IBM France. One of my jobs involved renewing the lease. From the papers in my office, it seemed that the founder of IBM, T J Watson Senior, convinced that Germany would win the war, had purchased it in 1941 before the US entered the war with the intention of using it as the European Headquarters building for IBM. After the war, when the German foreign property administrator released the building in the Place Vendôme, IBM France settled in to it and IBM Europe set itself up in the Cité du Retiro. IBM was unusual in having its headquarters in Paris: most multinationals had headquarters in Geneva, Brussels or London.

Little by little, my American boss allowed me to handle minor legal matters arising in the smaller European and Middle Eastern subsidiaries of IBM. First, I went to Iceland with instructions to replace the existing IBM agent by an IBM branch or, preferably, a wholly owned subsidiary. I remembered that at university I had known an Icelandic girl. She had since married an Icelander and returned home. I neither knew where she lived nor her married name. I sent an airmail letter, addressing it to 'Thorey Gudmansdottir (now married), born in Akureyri, Iceland', telling her of my arrival. There was no reply, but she was at the airport to meet me. The letter had been delivered to her without delay in the Westman Islands, where she lived. Later, I travelled to Israel and the Lebanon. The contrast between them was striking. Everyone seemed to go to bed before ten o'clock in Israel, but nobody seemed to go to bed at all in Beirut. The Casino was in full swing all night and one could dance until dawn at the Caves du Roi. There was a certain tension in the air. The army and police were much in evidence at night, but people were charming and there was little sign of the trouble to come.

There was contractual work too. For example, when my boss was away, I received a call from Denmark to go there to negotiate a contract for the rental of an airline reservation system for SAS. I did not know that I had to have authority to change the standard contract. I ought to have consulted the worldwide IBM HQ in New York. Thank goodness for my ignorance, though, because this contract became the IBM standard for real time business applications, and was the form used for the Pan Am reservation system in the US and the Air France system in Europe. But I was never again allowed to invent a new contract. IBM was dominant enough to impose its standard form on all its customers, other than the US and some other governments.

A lot of time was spent behind the Iron Curtain closing down IBM businesses that pre-dated the communist revolutions, and setting up new relationships with local enterprises. I got to know Yugoslavia, Czechoslovakia and Hungary quite well. Their governments were desperate to obtain up-to-date IBM equipment. We were happy to sell to them, but the US State Department was reluctant to grant licences. Sometimes we could bargain with both the US State Department and the Communist Governments. For example, we managed to persuade the US authorities to allow us to sell a computer to the Hungarian Government. In return, we persuaded the Hungarian Government to release the former IBM General Manager from prison, where he was being held on espionage charges. I remember visiting Hungary for the first time and being shown into the office of the Minister of Economy and Trade. 'Ah, gentlemen,' he said, 'we have a problem in this country. In order to have a successful socialist economy one needs the support of 5 per cent of the population. We have lost that support.'

It always seemed to be midwinter in Eastern Europe, probably because the Eastern Europeans liked to come to see us in Paris in the spring and summer. I would go off to Yugoslavia or Hungary with the Regional Manager, a hard-drinking American. We would be accompanied by the Chairman of IBM Austria, a distinguished elderly man, who was a baron of the Austro-Hungarian Empire and looked the part. He dressed in a sable fur hat and sported a long fur-lined coat which came down to his ankles. He was the epitome of the aristocrat and the communists loved him for it. We got the best service because of him. I remember a restaurant in Belgrade where he ordered oysters – the oysters were good in Yugoslavia because Tito liked them and had an island in the Aegean Sea set aside for their culture. The Baron called for crayfish. A large one was carried in by the waiter and set before him. He opened it up with both hands and carefully sniffed it. Then, he sent for all the crayfish the kitchen contained, sniffed them one by one, and chose the best. He had great style. The American Regional Manager cannot be said to have had any style at all. He got me into trouble in Prague by inviting me to the hotel nightclub after dinner and ordering champagne and drinks for everyone, including the orchestra and the bar girls. I discovered, on leaving the hotel, that the bill had been charged to my account, and this took some explaining to my boss back in Paris.

My work at IBM involved a lot of travel. In those days the European Community was in its infancy. At every frontier, even within the Community, there were vigilant customs officers whose sole function seemed to be checking to see that people did not exceed their duty-free spirit allowances. They always stopped me and I was frequently searched. I remember arriving in New York on the old *Queen Elizabeth*. On the quay the US Customs official went so far as to squeeze out a tube of toothpaste. After some years of this harassment, I decided to find out why it was happening. On my arrival at Heathrow I chose an older and apparently sympathetic customs officer. 'Why am I picked out wherever I go?' I asked. 'Well, sir,' he hesitated, 'you look rich, you see – but then again you don't look as if you were born to it!'

Nowadays, the work ethic is strong and people keep the most horrendous hours. I sometimes wonder whether we did the same. I cannot quite remember. We always seemed to have time for fun, but the hours could be long. Negotiations with the Eastern Europeans were particularly lengthy, perhaps because they had little power to take decisions themselves and had to refer back to the relevant minister. We, too, needed to obtain clearance from our own headquarters in New York. I remember participating in negotiations with the Yugoslavs in Paris. It was three o'clock in the morning. We were getting nowhere. The door opened and there was

Pitche, who came into the room and demanded her husband. The meeting broke up and we all went back to our hotels or homes. Everyone said, next day, how lucky I was to have such a wife.

One day, the Planning Director of IBM Europe came to my office. He explained that he was fully informed of IBM's plans for expansion across Europe. The projected growth was considerable, and he and four of his colleagues had seen that there was a business opportunity to be seized. They thought that they should start a company and build hotels everywhere where the Corporation planned a major factory or laboratory. The hotels would obtain at least fifty per cent occupancy from IBM visitors alone and the hotel company would have the advantage of benefiting from this early knowledge of the Corporation's intentions. He wanted to know whether I thought that such a project could be considered an inappropriate exploitation of insider information. I asked to be given the weekend to think it over and then wrote an opinion confirming that they were, of course, using inside information but that this was not against the interests of IBM. Indeed, the created facilities would positively assist the development of the company. A couple of weeks later he came back to me, thanked me, and offered a place in the syndicate for $50,000. I refused because I thought that my opinion then might be thought to have been self-interested. In any event, even if I had been tempted, I did not have $50,000. So I missed my chance of being a director and part owner of the Novotel chain.

Foreign assignment: London

IBM was growing fast and not all the employees were able to keep up. There was an example of this in the UK, where the Company Secretary woke up one Sunday morning in 1965 to find his job advertised in *The Times*. He rang me and we plotted a solution. I would go to London for a couple of years and he would come to Paris for training. A good way to make money in international companies has long been to go on international assignment, receiving allowances and paying little tax. There was a real piquancy in the thought of being sent to my own country on foreign assignment. Before we left for London, Pitche and I happened to go to a party at

the British Embassy. There, we met Chloë and Crispin Tickell. Chloë heard someone behind her say, 'Did you know that the Blackburns are going to London?' She
turned round and said, 'Tell them to rent my house.' We were introduced and, in
due course, we rented their house in Abercorn Place in St John's Wood. In this
way, Chloë became our landlady when we went to London. Little did I suspect
then that she would become my wife, twenty years later.

Because I had met Pitche in France, I had always spoken French to her and to
my sons. We arrived in London as a French-speaking family and this continued.
Alexander was nearly three years old, but did not speak a word of English. With
some misgivings, we sent him off to a local nursery school. He came back on the first
day and slipped up to his room without saying a word. We thought that he must
be in shock because he could not understand what was going on at the school,
so we crept up the stairs and listened at his door, only to hear a little voice saying,
'Fook, Fluck, Flook.' He was fine, just practising his vocabulary for the next day.

There was a shock awaiting me at IBM UK. About six months before, I had been
asked to go to see the IBM Northern Europe Regional Manager, who had his office
in London. When I arrived he was accompanied by the Managing Director of
IBM UK. They asked me to investigate a marketing matter in which IBM UK
had apparently made commitments to a customer beyond company policy and
without authority. It was not the kind of role that I enjoyed, but I did the job with
a fairly light heart because I knew none of the people involved. I made my report
to the effect that company policy had been breached and that the person responsible was the Northern District Manager of IBM UK, a certain Edwin Nixon. At a
kangaroo court in Paris and in front of Edwin Nixon, I presented my conclusions
to the President of IBM Europe. Months later, taking up my new job in London,
I found that the Managing Director of the UK Company had left and had been
replaced by Edwin Nixon. He had the tact never to mention our previous meeting.

The headquarters of IBM UK were then at 101 Wigmore Street in the West
End, but the company had grown out of the space available there and plans were
being made to move to a rather ugly building in Chiswick, above Gunnersbury

tube station. On taking up my job in Wigmore Street, I was appalled by the state of the legal department. It was a real mess, with papers everywhere and bulging filing cabinets. When I opened the safe, presumably containing the most important documents relating to the company, the papers fell out on top of me. When I taxed my predecessor's secretary with the situation, she wept and protested that she had tried to clear things up, but had received no support or authority to act. We decided to stay late every evening, put on old clothes, and throw out the surplus paper. For some weeks we had a wonderful time, while my predecessor, who had not yet left for Paris, hung around, wringing his hands and saying that disaster would occur because we were clearing out essential records. In fact, we were never asked for a document that we could not find, and the offices became tidy and the work easier.

UK Executive

My new bosses in the UK seemed satisfied and, after two years, they offered promotion to stay on in England rather than return to France. After much hesitation, we decided to remain in London. By this time the move of the headquarters to Gunnersbury had taken place. By becoming a local employee, I relinquished the right to have my rent paid by the company. We had to find somewhere to live other than Abercorn Place, which in any event was not at all convenient for Chiswick. I took Pitche to Strand-on-the-Green, a lovely spot overlooking the Thames and within walking distance of the new offices. I proposed that we should buy one of the beautiful Georgian houses on the towpath. Pitche looked around and said, 'It's very nice, I suppose, but I don't like the country.' We moved out of Abercorn Place, bought a more central, newly built Wates house in Woodsford Square, Holland Park and the boys started at the French Lycée.

The Real Estate and Construction department was added to the Legal and Company Secretarial departments. I was to have fun building factories, laboratories and offices to accommodate a net increase in personnel of over 1,000 per year. Between the 1960s and 1980s, IBM UK grew from 8,000 to 20,000 employees. I told my mother of my promotion and of my pleasure at moving from being just a lawyer to being accepted into general management. She looked worried. 'So you are no longer the head lawyer?' she said, dubiously. 'No, Mother,' I said. 'Look at it this way: if the top dozen managers of the company were to be sent to prison, I would be one of them.' 'Oh,' she said, 'don't take the job, Billie.'

One of the problems then for a company growing so fast was that we were not allowed to expand anywhere near to London. It was firm government policy, backed with appropriate powers, to oblige companies to move to the provinces. I spent a lot of time negotiating with the relevant government department in an effort to obtain permission to build somewhere nearer to London than, say, Manchester Airport. Our greatest problem was our need for an administrative headquarters. In the end we bought the edge of Portsmouth harbour, where a motorway had left a belt of shallow water protected from the sea. We got Dutch engineers to dry out the land, which was slightly under sea level. They made a polder, building a large lake and installing a permanent pump to keep the land dry, and we designed a building for 5,000 employees. Eddie Nixon came into my office one morning and said, 'How many cars will we have on the site?' 'About 4,000 or possibly more,' I replied. He shook his head and said, 'And they will all be below sea level?'

One day we were inspecting the plans for the new administrative HQ at Portsmouth and I noticed that there were many temporary caravan-type buildings. I asked why we needed these and was told that they were to house the architects, surveyors and builders while the permanent building was going up. Looking at the budget, I saw that they would cost a considerable sum over five years. I then asked whether we could get an architect to design a temporary building for less than the total budget. We hired a young unknown architect called Norman Foster for the job and he got a prize for the building. It is still there – so much for 'temporary'. Much later, I asked the now famous Sir Norman Foster whether I might tell this story and he said, 'It's not quite as I remember it, but I will never deny it.'

We received a stream of requests for corporate support from charities and artistic organisations. Handling them was time-consuming. At board meetings, donations were a standing item on the agenda and board members pleaded for their favourites. One day I rang up the Arts Council and asked them if they would accept a substantial yearly contribution to their work from IBM. They replied that they were a government body, with no association or link to the private sector. It took some effort to persuade them that they could take our money. I suggested that there must be things that they would love to do, but for which they did not have sufficient resources. This they admitted to be true and they were in the end persuaded to accept a yearly contribution. The first donation was used to open the Serpentine Gallery in Hyde Park. We were then able to refer all requests for artistic and cultural support to the Arts Council, and remove charitable contributions from the Board's Agenda.

The Labour Government controlled industry, or tried to. Each sector had its sponsoring ministry and our minister, the Minister of Technology, was Tony Benn. In an endeavour to control inflation, price increases had to be approved by the ministry. IBM decided to increase prices across Europe and our request for permission to

Alexander and Jimmy on the boat with Le Canadel in the background

follow suit was refused. We went to see Tony Benn. Eddie Nixon explained what we wanted, while Benn drank tea from his pint mug. The minister was very polite but turned us down, saying that he could not give permission. Such a price increase would be against government policy. I said, speaking probably out of turn and certainly without authority, that his decision would have two unfortunate consequences. First, it would mean that our British competitor, ICL, would suffer increased competition. Secondly, as we were ourselves in competition for US investment with the IBM subsidiaries elsewhere in Europe, we would be less profitable and have less chance of drawing capital investment to the UK. Benn's reaction was violent. 'I refuse to react to threats,' he said. 'You are threatening me.' We left and drove to the Headquarters of ICL on Putney Bridge. Stalking in, we demanded to see the Managing Director, Arthur Humphreys. We were shown into his smoke-filled office. 'Hello, Eddie,' he said. Turning to me, he said, 'You're the youngest – you can serve the whisky.' Even Arthur Humphreys could not get Tony Benn to change his mind. In the end, we appealed to the Prices and Income Board and got authorisation for a price increase from them – but that is another story.

Although I missed Paris, I enjoyed being in the UK – in part because I was able to play a greater role in local life. For example, I joined the Commerce and Industry Group of the Law Society and became its Vice-Chairman. I was awarded a Sloan Fellowship to go to Business School for a year. The choice was between MIT, Stamford and London. We chose London because we thought it would be fun to remain at home on an IBM salary. In the end I never went because of pressure of work. Pitche settled down well in London, although she lived mainly within the French community. She learned to cook, taking lessons at the Cordon Bleu school in Marylebone Lane, and she always had an au pair for the children. My job did not involve much travel so I was almost always at home.[11] I played golf most

11 I had techniques to limit travel to the US or to render it enjoyable. The first was to suggest that the person might like to come to Europe, normally accepted with enthusiasm. The second, if this failed, was to propose that the meeting take place on a Monday or Tuesday afternoon in New York – thus allowing for a weekend in Bermuda.

weekends, but started early so as to be home for lunch and spend the rest of the day with the boys. They went with Pitche to France to stay with her family for most holidays and I went over to Belloy or to Le Canadel when I could. We went skiing, but otherwise we never went on a holiday away from my parents-in-law until 1973, when we rented a villa in Tangiers. I was forty by then, so family independence came late.

CHAPTER 10

Far from the centre of power

IBM held a virtual monopoly in the data processing market and, rather like Microsoft today, was suspected of abusing its dominant position. In particular, the practice of 'bundling' hardware and software so that customers could not buy one without the other was considered a possible abuse. The US authorities had started an anti-trust case against IBM Corporation and it was consequently thought that the European Community competition authorities would start an action against IBM in Europe. IBM employed over 100,000 people in Europe: it was a very important market for us. It was decided that we should set up a company in Brussels to monitor the activities of the European Community and to co-ordinate IBM's response to all governmental and inter-governmental issues, including competition law. I was offered the job of Managing Director of the IBM European Office in Brussels and accepted with alacrity. This surprised my colleagues in the UK. They thought that being an executive of IBM UK was a bigger and better job. I, however, was delighted because I was much more independent and reported directly to IBM Europe. I could use my French and, being on assignment, I was better paid.

At first, the company was housed in the headquarters of IBM Belgium situated in the centre of Brussels, on the Rue Royale – opposite the war memorial. I soon learned that Belgium was a divided country. Pointing to the flame at the bottom of the war memorial column, and searching for something to say, I asked the Belgian showing me around whether it marked the tomb of the Unknown Soldier. 'Certainly not,' he replied huffily. 'That is the tomb of the Flemish Soldier.' 'Really?' said I. 'Of course,' he insisted. 'If he had been a Walloon, he would have been known.' Later we moved to offices in the Avenue Louise and eventually to the International Education Centre of IBM in the forest of La Hulpe south of Brussels. The building had a large sculpture by Henry Moore in the form of a sundial at the entrance. This had been purchased from either *The Times* or the *Observer* newspaper. I cannot remember which. It had been shipped over at dead of night from the UK because nobody was really sure which newspaper company did own it.

We settled into a pleasant house next to the Russian Church in Uccle, a French-speaking suburb of Brussels. The boys went to the French Lycée, and we proceeded to enjoy the best years of our lives. I had access to the top management of IBM in Europe and the US. I was encouraged to get to know key people in the European Community institutions. I seemed to have an infinite expense account. I defined and then managed key issues affecting IBM and co-ordinated the activities of the government-relations staffs in the subsidiary IBM companies of Europe, Africa and the Middle East. Having gone on assignment to Brussels for three years, I stayed eight. This was really far too long and did not help my career. However, I did love my time in Brussels and have no regrets.

After much reflection and discussion, we decided to send the boys to Ampleforth, a Catholic boarding school in the North Riding of Yorkshire. Dom Maurus, the Benedictine priest who had turned up at our wedding, had written, after Alexander's birth, to assure us that places would be made available. We thought that a move from the French system to the British would give the boys an advantage in later life. Another consideration was that IBM would pay the fees, so long as I remained on assignment. Also, Pitche had been educated at an English boarding school and felt that she would like her sons to follow the same path. Alexander hated the place, but Jimmy settled down well. There was a frequent night boat from Zeebrugge to Hull, making travel to and from school at the beginning and end of term relatively easy.

We enjoyed the quality of life in Brussels. In fact I think that I would prefer to live in Brussels rather than in either Paris or London. We went to the opera regularly and were often invited to dinner parties. My work was interesting and stimulating. We held off anti-trust litigation by the European Commission for many years and, when, eventually, we were attacked for abuse of our dominant position we were prepared for it, and were able to settle the case satisfactorily. I suppose that I fitted into Brussels life a little more easily than Pitche. The Belgians have a language complex vis-à-vis the French, but a French-speaking Englishman is well received. We became members of the Royal Golf Club of Belgium and met many Belgians through golf. Pitche became the president of a club for the wives of senior officials of the institutions of the European Community and through that group we made many more friends.

The best thing about Brussels was the number of interesting people living there. It housed the headquarters of many international companies. My friend Ronnie Lagden, with whom I played golf most weekends, ran the European operations of Quaker Oats. There were people connected with the headquarters of NATO and plenty associated in some way with the European Community. The protocol services of the Belgian government worked hard sorting out whether, for example, a European Commissioner had precedence over a NATO General. Many people came to Brussels and were accessible in a way that they might not have been in their own country. I had tea with Mitterand and got to know Ted Heath quite well, at least well enough for him to invite us to lunch in Salisbury on my return to the UK. The 'knitting' factor was evident in Brussels. For example, Sir Christopher Soames was a Commisioner. Earlier, when Ambassador in Paris, he and his wife, Mary, had rented Le Canadel and I had taken Mary, Churchill's daughter, to dinner in St Tropez. Roy Jenkins was President of the Commission and his head of cabinet was Crispin Tickell, recently divorced from his wife, Chloë, who was to become my wife in the not so distant future. Our good friends included two English couples, Sydney and Judy Freedman and John and Sue Kenchington. Both were to divorce. Sydney Freedman was to marry Nadia who, before I introduced her to Sydney, helped in the 1980s to open Theodore Goddard's Brussels office. Judy married John Kenchington, divorced him, and then, when he became ill, returned to nurse him until he died.

Not everyone thought that what I was doing in Brussels was important. Many of my IBM colleagues thought that I had chosen the soft option and should have remained in the operational heart of the Company. People in the European Commission sometimes referred to me as the 'IBM spy'. However, I thought that I was doing vital work, key to the future success of IBM. If I had had any doubts, they would have been reinforced after my return to the UK. I met Lord Cockfield, one of the British Commissioners appointed by Mrs Thatcher, with responsibility for the Internal Market. He was at the Law Society to give the Fletcher Lecture and Richard Gaskell, the President, had asked him to the Presidential flat in Carey Street. Arthur Cockfield was reminiscing about Brussels. I asked him whether he had enjoyed his time there, adding that I had greatly enjoyed my eight years. Addressing the room in general, he said, 'Anyone who enjoyed himself in Brussels must have been very far from the centre of power.'

CHAPTER 11

Stormy weather

After eight most enjoyable years on the far edges of power in Brussels, I was transferred to Paris. On arrival, I found that I was much out of favour. There was no real job for me in the European Headquarters. I was given a nice title and a pleasant office and attached to the legal department. This was not demotion exactly, but I felt that my career was stagnating. For the first time, I found myself underemployed. I would go to my club to practise yoga and I learned to play bridge. My golf improved, but I was miserable. When a position came up in the UK, I jumped at the chance to get away.

IBM UK had grown large, employing over 20,000 people. I was appointed Manager of Business Practices, with responsibility for contracts and negotiations with customers and suppliers. The job was in Portsmouth, the new administrative headquarters of the British company. I may have been responsible for its design, but I did not particularly appreciate the working environment of the building. There was nowhere to go except for a walk around the lake at lunchtime and nobody to see except IBM colleagues. One good thing was that I had a place on the IBM UK Management Committee, which met every Friday to take the operating decisions for the IBM UK Group. I participated as a member of the Committee, but because of my legal background, I was also asked to record its conclusions. There were no minutes, fortunately, but action points, due dates, and the person responsible were defined and recorded. Then, over the weekend, I checked my notes and ensured that the relevant decisions appeared on each divisional director's desk by nine o'clock on Monday morning. With email technology, this would now be easy, but it required a lot of effort then and spoiled the weekends.

At one of the Management Committee meetings, the Director of Manufacturing announced that he had succeeded in persuading our American management to assemble the new Personal Computer at Greenock in Scotland. This would ensure full employment at the factory for a number of years. He was congratulated. Then the Director of Research and Development said that he hoped that he would not be asked for resources to assist in the development of the operating system required for the machine. He said that all his software people were fully stretched, working on programming projects for major customers, such as banks and insurance companies. He reminded the Committee that forty per cent of our revenue came from our ten biggest customers. The Director of Manufacturing said that there was no problem. A deal had been struck with a little software company, Microsoft, run by a young man called Bill Gates. Free of charge, he would develop an operating system called MS/DOS, a simplified version of DOS. IBM and Microsoft would each have unrestricted use of the system, so it was an excellent deal for both parties. We nodded our heads sagely. This was the huge error of judgment that came near to destroying IBM and made Bill Gates, the founder of Microsoft, the richest man in the world. Nobody, at that time, foresaw the immense success of the personal computer.

My office was in the headquarters building in Havant at the entrance to Portsmouth, which is, in effect, an island connected to the mainland by a single road. To be within easy reach, we settled in Winchester, renting the Bell House, in St Swithin's Street, next to the Cathedral Close. I liked the city and the house, but Pitche felt isolated away from London. Pitche, like most Parisian women, was not attracted to either provincial or country life. She instinctively felt that being away from the capital was an admission of failure. So we bought a house in the New Kings Road in Fulham from John and Sue Kenchington. The drive to Portsmouth from London took two hours, so I could not always get back from Portsmouth to London. I rented a room, which I could use during the week, from Anna and Stephen Langton, friends who lived near Petersfield. Even so, commuting between London and Portsmouth was a strain.

Tragically, Pitche had developed cancer during our time in Brussels. She was operated on in Paris and colostomised. Initially she recovered well. In fact, she became more beautiful than she had ever been and was positively radiant. She became a leading light in the French Association for the Colostomised and spoke of her experiences to many groups of patients. She was even asked to make the Christmas charitable appeal on French television, and she spoke wonderfully, just before the President of the Republic. She was dressed for the occasion by Chanel, who lent her a beautiful blouse, and I thought that it would be nice to buy it for her as a memento. When I went to the shop, however, the manageress explained that the blouse was 'couture', meaning that it was unique. The price was over £2,000, so Pitche never received her present.

Her health deteriorated while we were on holiday in Le Canadel in the summer of 1983. The cancer had moved to the liver. There was no hope. The surgeons operated in Paris and removed part of the liver to give her some time, for she was eager to live as long as possible. IBM behaved superbly. They transferred me to Paris with full allowances and gave me time off for as long as necessary to nurse Pitche. We installed ourselves in Belloy for the winter and she died there, after going into a coma, in the spring of 1984. Odette Wallut, Pitche's aunt, was wonderful. She took Pitche into her Paris flat at the beginning of her illness and looked after her with devotion. I will always be grateful to her. She is certainly someone to turn to in a crisis. André also was a support; he suffered, but did not complain. After Pitche's death he seemed to feel that he had nothing more to live for. He became deeply depressed and died of heart failure, sitting up in bed. Pitche died in March 1984 and André in August 1985.

On my return to the UK without Pitche and to IBM UK, I found that I was mentally and physically exhausted. Things had changed during my absence. My old boss Eddie Nixon had become Chairman and Chief Executive. There was a new General Manager, a man for whom I had little respect and who treated me fairly but coldly. As I had saved some money in Brussels, it seemed to me that I could, by renouncing

riches and taking a very reduced pension, just about afford to take early retirement.
I was fifty-two. It was almost unknown for anybody to leave IBM voluntarily at
the time, so I was able to negotiate generous terms. The terms were in fact more
generous than the Personnel Director realised. As I had spent the majority of my
career outside the UK, a Finance Act specified that any cash payment on retirement
was entirely untaxed. The company deducted tax on the amount over £25,000 but
then had to pay that to me and not to the Revenue.

On retirement, I found that I was not weaned from a regular working life, nor
from the need to go to an office. I contacted my old firm, Theodore Goddard, and
they took me on in London as a consultant. They were surprised, I think, that I
was not interested in processing client work or in becoming a partner. All I wanted
was an office as a base from which to operate, and something interesting to do. I
worked as a project manager: doing for the senior partner things he did not have the
time to do himself. I helped to change the image of the firm, set up a marketing
department, instigate a strategic plan and open a Brussels Office.

CHAPTER 12

Professional antics

In 1978 I was sitting at my desk in Brussels when the phone rang. It was John Bowron, then Secretary-General of the Law Society. 'I suppose you know why I am calling you?' he said. 'I have no idea,' I replied, 'but I can't be in trouble because I have no client money to steal – indeed I have no clients to steal it from.' 'It's not that, we want you to join the Council,' he replied. 'It's impossible,' I explained. 'I'm not in legal practice, I'm not working as a lawyer in IBM, and I live in Brussels.' 'The three reasons why we want you,' he said. Once appointed, I remained a co-opted member of the Law Society Council for seventeen years.

While living abroad, I slipped over to London for Council meetings every month. There were often formal dinners arranged to coincide with them. I got so fed up having to carry over a dinner jacket that I bought another and kept it in London. To keep expenses to the minimum, the Law Society arranged membership of the RAC, where I could stay. I became a member of the Law Reform Committee – I have no idea why. I was certainly not consulted, knew little about the law, and almost nothing about its reform. This did not matter because the secretary did all the work. He was the brilliantly intelligent Hamish Adamson, who later added international matters to his responsibilities. In due course I was given a committee to chair. This was the Law Office Management and Technology Committee, far more in my line. We tried to introduce technology to the profession and had some success in the development of financial and billing systems for law firms. I did, however, make a big mistake by backing an early version of email, BT Gold. It was not taken up by the profession, and even now I am still teased about it by those of my colleagues who have long memories and a nose for failure.

After I left IBM, I had more time to spare for professional matters. The Council made me Chairman of the International Committee and its representative on the UK Delegation to the European Bar Council (the CCBE). Unlike almost all of my Council colleagues, who were obliged to combine professional matters with full-time practice, I had time to concentrate on these roles. I was particularly fascinated by the work of the CCBE. John Young, my predecessor as Chairman, had been the head of the UK Delegation, doing excellent work moulding the different elements of the delegation into a coherent body.[12] I arrived when the CCBE had just adopted a common code of conduct for all lawyers in the European Community, applying to cross-border legal practice. Together with Hamish Adamson, who acted as secretary of the UK Delegation, I was able to play a role in the next major achievement.

Establishment

For many years, the professions had been divided on whether and, if so, how European lawyers could establish themselves and their firms in each other's jurisdictions. The French delegation, supported by the Spanish, Italian, Belgian and Luxembourg Bars, wanted a regime whereby every lawyer working abroad, on anything other than a temporary basis, would be obliged to become a member of the local Bar. They were prepared to make entry to the Bar easy, but they did not want a plethora of different kinds of lawyers in their countries, all subject to different disciplinary regimes and rules of conduct. The British, supported by the Dutch, the Scandinavians and, eventually, the Germans, were protective of their title and did not want anyone who was not fully qualified to be able to practise in their countries using a reserved title, for example, that of solicitor or *Rechtsanwalt*. They

---

12 Although English solicitors compose over eighty per cent of the UK legal profession by number, they are an equal sixth part of the UK Delegation to the CCBE. The other five are the English, Scottish and Northern Irish Bars and the Scottish and Northern Irish Law Societies.

were, however, prepared to allow foreign lawyers to establish themselves under their home title and to practise freely, so long as they avoided 'reserved activities' such as court work or conveyancing. As a French Judge at the European Court, André Potocki, once said, 'If I understand correctly, in France you can do anything, so long as you call yourself an *avocat*, and in England you can do almost everything, so long as you do not call yourself a solicitor.'

Positions were entrenched and defended with passion. The most influential member of the French delegation was the head of the Paris Bar, Georges Flecheux. Georges has become one of my greatest friends, but at my first meeting of the CCBE in Copenhagen he was the enemy. As at all CCBE meetings, spouses were invited for the social occasions. We sat across the table from each other at lunch. Next to me was Madame de Ricci, the wife of the CCBE President. Georges and I had a passionate discussion. It was fascinating for us, but it did not please Madame de Ricci who stormed out of the room and had to be placated. We apologised for our bad manners, but were not forgiven.

The French position had some merit, but it was impossible to persuade my British colleagues in Paris and Brussels that it was reasonable to register with the local Bar and accept a measure of local discipline. They argued fiercely that the meaning of the free movement provisions of the European Community Treaty meant that English firms could establish themselves throughout the Community without regard to the local legal profession. To break the deadlock with our colleagues on the Continent, we set up a series of consultative meetings with their senior partners in London. Hamish Adamson called these the meetings of the 'Moguls'. The Moguls saw the larger picture and, with their support, we were able to change the British position and accept local registration and discipline. This was, of course, on condition that the right to practise under home title was retained.

Then we had to persuade our Latin colleagues, in particular the French, to accept a compromise. If they registered with and submitted to the discipline and professional rules of the local Bar or Law Society, could European colleagues have the right to practise under their home titles without becoming local lawyers?

My French language ability helped us to persuade Georges Flecheux. A compromise was reached. In Barcelona, the French Delegation changed its view and in Lisbon there was a majority for an Establishment Directive. After eighteen years of negotiation, we struck a deal. The southern European Bars had got part of what they wanted: registration, local discipline and local professional rules. We had got the free right of establishment under our home title. Unlike the US where, for example, a New York lawyer cannot practise in Florida, European lawyers are now free to practise throughout the European Union. The Luxembourg Bar never accepted the deal and took the matter to the European Court. They lost. Now settled at last in the European Union, this issue is not resolved globally and my successors are still trying to deal with it. I understand that the arguments have hardly changed.

CCBE meetings were sometimes frustrating for those of us who wished to make progress on professional matters. Spouses were expected to attend a social programme. The local Bar entertained the delegates with trips, lunches and formal dinners, although black tie was never worn. Looking back, I see that there was a purpose in all this socialising. We got to know each other well. We, and our spouses, made lasting friendships. The local Bar became involved in the process. Compromises were worked out over long meals drowned in excellent wine. Chloë, my sculptor wife, produced a medal for the CCBE that is now presented to the great and the good of the law around Europe. The Irish taught us to sing and the Greeks and Catalonians taught us to dance. The fun helped us all to come out of our trenches and to fraternise.

Junketing

The International Committee was not concerned with European affairs alone. I arrived at a moment of expansion in international matters. To cope, I applied my legal speciality, delegation. Each member of the Committee took responsibility for a subject and set up a working party to handle it. Relations with the notaries, was one such. I remember accompanying the chairman of our notarial working party to see the Paris notaries. Their president turned out to be a neighbour in Le Canadel. It was the first time we had seen each other dressed for the city. He took me aside. 'How much does a partner in one of your large City firms take home?' he asked. 'It depends on the firm and their seniority,' I replied. 'Between one and four hundred thousand pounds, I suppose.' 'Less than us then,' he said.

Norman Bonham Carter took responsibility for relations with China. These were important because of the number of English solicitors in Hong Kong and the impending return of the Colony to China. It was essential to cultivate good relations with the Chinese Ministry of Justice and the Chinese Bar. He did the job wonderfully, taking into his home young Chinese lawyers who were on the British Council Young Lawyers programme. We arranged for the head of the Chinese Bar, whom we nicknamed 'Sue You', to be invited the Opening of the Legal Year. It was interesting to see him at the service in Westminster Abbey, standing out among the finery of the Bar and the Judiciary in his Mao suit. At the Lord Chancellor's Breakfast,[13] the President of the Scottish Law Society, dressed in full Highland regalia, with a light blue robe and chain of office, came up and accused me of typical English bad manners because Mr Sue You was standing alone. We went over to him. The ebullient Scot launched into a conversation to the effect that Sue You and he had much in common, because they were both foreigners. It was the opening of the English Legal Year and he was not English, but a Scot. The proof was that he was wearing the kilt. Mr Sue You brightened up at this and, through the interpreter, said that they also in China had ethnic minorities, some of which wore skirts.

Eastern Europe merited its own working party under Stephen Rayner because our firms were anxious to expand into that market. My friend Diana Guy, the Chair of the Solicitors' European Group, took over responsibility for the 1992 Awareness Campaign. We have forgotten now what that was about, but it concerned the opening of the Single European Market and its importance for the profession. I managed to delegate almost everything other than CCBE affairs. International Committee meetings came to consist of reports on each subject presented by the

13   The reception held in Westminster Hall after the service in Westminster Abbey.

person responsible. It was efficient and very pleasant for me as Chairman, but hard work for the staff, having to service the working parties as well as the Committee. We became a popular committee and influential Council members wanted to join us.

My Achilles heel was human rights. I found myself Chair of the International Human Rights Sub-committee. The membership was composed largely of human rights zealots. Whatever the Law Society did, they wanted more. For example, if the President wrote a letter in support of an imprisoned lawyer, the committee members would want the Law Society to send a delegation. If a delegation was sent, it was either not large enough or was composed of the wrong people. It was clear that I was no expert in the field. I became extremely uncomfortable with the methods of argument used by some of the members. They seemed to be saying that if I did not agree with them totally and without reservation, I was evil. We had lively sessions, culminating at one point in a walkout. There was nothing I could do except admit failure. I passed the reins of the Sub-committee to David Jefferson, a Council Member with good anti-establishment credentials. He was an immediate success and the Sub-committee did excellent work. This disagreeable experience taught me a lesson and I learned what I could about human rights. When, later, I became Chairman of the British Council Law Advisory Committee, which is much concerned with international human rights, I was able to write articles and make speeches on the subject with some confidence.

Part of the attraction of the International Committee was, of course, the prospect of foreign travel. This was certainly why some Council members wanted to join. I was quite relaxed about whether I travelled or not. IBM had provided me with an excess of travel opportunities. It was, of course, necessary to go to the CCBE meetings, held fairly frequently in various European countries, from Denmark to Cyprus. Because it was francophone, I took as another fief the International Union of Lawyers, the French-inspired rival to the International Bar Association. I remember enjoyable, but extremely disorganised, meetings in Mexico and Quebec. I left my predecessor, John Young, to represent the Law Society at IBA meetings and I encouraged the chairs of the working parties to travel as necessary.

Just before the uprising in Tiananmen Square, we had a fantastic trip to China with a large delegation representing the European Bar. It was then that I discovered that Norman Bonham Carter, the Chairman of the International Committee's China Working Party, had become famous. Everywhere we went they asked, 'Where is Mr Bonham Carter, please?' We dined twice in the Great Hall of the People and visited the statues of the warriors and the Great Wall. Our Attorney General, Sir Patrick Mayhew, and a number of others queued to make speeches. On the stroke of nine, all the Chinese stood up, pocketed the fruit and left without saying good-bye, as if a secret signal had been given and received.

We travelled to Shanghai, which had not yet started its enormous development. There was no underground system and I have never experienced a more crowded place. The Bund looked just like Liverpool. We ate wonderfully well in Canton and rather badly elsewhere – I never want to see a sea cucumber again. We travelled in tired military planes made in Russia or in a convoy of coaches with police out-riders, who drove everyone else off the road using their sirens. We thought we were important until, occasionally, we were, in our turn, driven off the road by another more prestigious cavalcade. The coaches were divided by language. There were French-speaking coaches and English-speaking coaches. Once, a nice Belgian couple asked whether they might join our coach because they could not stand the grumbling in the French coach. At the end of the trip we went by train from Canton to Hong Kong. The contrast between the poverty of China and the prosperity of Hong Kong was most striking.

Apotheosis

One thing leads to another. An interest in international legal matters, combined with a knowledge of French, got me involved in the Franco-British Lawyers' Association, of which I later became President. To run the Society I co-operated with Michael Butcher, a lawyer who also had a background in industry. He had worked at Esso and had been Secretary of the Channel Tunnel Company, moving on to Vivendi. We applied the management techniques that we had been taught in commerce to the fledgling organisation, and it flourished. We took no credit for its formation. This was the work of a legal adviser to the French Embassy in London, Michel Koenig, and of his assistant George Cumming. When I handed over the Presidency of the Society to Myriam Ezratty, First President of the Paris Court of Appeal, I wrote an article in the journal of the Society in which I paid tribute to Michel Koenig. Imagine my surprise when I received a letter from George Cumming, a lecturer in the Bar's Training College, threatening a libel action because I had not mentioned him in my article. As a retirement present, I received the political novels of Trollope, published by the Trollope Society and beautifully inscribed.

Chairmanship of the Law Society International Committee involves membership of the British Council Law Advisory Committee. Eventually I succeeded Nicholas Philips, now Lord Phillips and the Master of the Rolls, to its chair. I was the first Chairman not to be or become a Law Lord, and the first solicitor. These activities led on to membership of the Franco-British Council, a bilateral governmental organisation, founded by Edward Heath and President Pompidou to improve relations between the two countries. My most recent appointment has been to the Advisory Council of the Entente Cordiale Scholarship programme, chaired by Roy Jenkins. In 1997 I was awarded the OBE and made a Chevalier of the Legion of Honour for work in the field of Franco-British relations, a rare double. The letter announcing the OBE made me very excited. I shouted the news to Chloë who calmed me down by saying, 'Isn't that a bit mere?' When I went to collect the medal at Buckingham Palace, I was told the Queen might say something, but that all conversation must stop as soon as she put out her hand. She asked how long I had been doing 'this good work'. Sensing an opportunity, I said about nine years and went on to say that the French thought that it was good work too – they had made me a Chevalier of the Legion of Honour. 'Oh,' she said, deadpan, and putting out her hand, 'how interesting.'

When the four years of the International Committee expired, I took the chair

Apotheosis – in Alma Square

of the Post Qualification Training Casework Committee. We administered the compulsory Continuing Professional Development scheme and helped introduce the study of management into solicitors' training. Most client complaints concern a lack of communication and management skills rather than poor-quality legal advice. When I left the Law Society, Trevor Boutall and I wrote *The Solicitors' Guide to Good Management*, which has become the set book on management for young solicitors. It is mainly composed of checklists, based upon either the National Management Standards or the Law Society's own Practice Management Standards. It is a melding of the two sets of standards, simplified to make them easy to assimilate. I cannot claim that the book contains much original thought. Only one page is entirely my own; I have reproduced it at the end of this memoir and it is, in effect, my testament.

To be the representative of the Trainee Solicitors on the Law Society Council is an interesting role. Because they were not yet qualified, the 14,000 trainees and law students did not have direct representation on the Council. However, they had the right to choose a Council member to represent them and defend their interests. They chose me, and I represented them for three years. I fought hard to oblige firms to provide proper standards of training and to pay decent minimum salaries. One year, to my delight, the National Committee of the Trainee Group was entirely composed of women. They taught me how to express myself with a certain amount of political correctness, but I have now largely forgotten the skill. I enjoyed one committee meeting in particular. They held it in the sauna of a hotel in Bristol and I was the only man present.

One great regret was that I never became Chairman of the Wine Committee. Norman Bonham Carter chaired it well and for many years. I had hoped to replace him when he retired. He rang me and said that he assumed that I expected to become Chairman. He went on to say that he had thought about it and I did know quite a lot about Bordeaux. However, he thought that my knowledge of Burgundy was scanty and I knew hardly anything about Port. He had therefore decided that John Aucott, a fellow Council member, would be better at the job. Everything Norman said was true, so I had nothing to complain about. We have remained good friends and he came to Alexander's wedding. John Aucott was excellent. At the first meeting that he chaired, he asked to be told the annual budget at our disposal. It was £14,000. 'It will have to be increased substantially,' he said. 'I spend more than that on wine at home, just for the family.'

You'll miss me when I've gone

I left the Law Society Council in 1995, and my departure coincided with a palace revolution in the profession. A pair of high street practitioners presented them-selves for election as President and Vice-President of the Council, in opposition to the candidates chosen by the Council in the traditional manner. The profession elected them President and Vice-President by a large majority. Their arrival in power did not cause my resignation, but it seemed to be the moment to leave. I had no sympathy with their aims. The man I admired was John Hayes, the Secretary-General of the Law Society, the former Chief Executive of Warwickshire, a brilliant administrator. I had been on the working party that chose him and he was clearly the outstanding candidate. Once hired, he fulfilled his promise.

Under John's guidance, the Law Society had become an efficient machine with excellent and devoted staff. It had forced the expansion of the Government's legal aid budget exponentially: to the point that it was effectively out of control, with all the money going to the profession. The UK has by far the largest legal aid budget in Europe, making us the envy of our continental colleagues. The profession had been liberated from its antique professional rules, forbidding advertising and marketing, and had been removed from the sterile world of restrictive practices. In an era in which the consumer is king, the Law Society had recognised that the profession served its own interests best by putting public interest first. Quality of entry into the profession had been assured by the introduction of minimum salaries for trainees. The examination system had been reformed, to place an emphasis on the skills needed to apply the law in practice. The Bar's monopoly of rights of audience in the high court was being effectively attacked and the morale of the Bar was low. The future seemed to be with solicitors rather than barristers.

However, the Law Society had, and still has, a fatal weakness. This is its failure to communicate its success to the profession and particularly to high street practitioners. Almost all the elected members of the Council have local Law Society backgrounds, and they believe that communication with local Law Societies is communication with the profession. In fact, local Law Societies have no better image with the profession than does the Law Society. They also believe that to place something in the pages of the *Law Society Gazette* keeps the profession informed. To maximise advertising revenue, the *Gazette* appears weekly and busy practitioners rarely open it, even if they generally claim to do so. Attempts were, of course, made to improve communication with the profession. Road-shows were sent out, but normally only local Law Society activists attended them. The profession generally was totally unaware that it had an excellent professional body. The situation was, and still is, made worse by the fact that the Law Society has two different roles that are frequently confused. In addition to being the association promoting the interests of the profession, it has disciplinary powers. The result is that many solicitors believe the Law Society to be the profession's policing authority rather than its friend.

There is another view of what happened. This is that the Law Society did communicate appropriately, but that the profession was not ready to accept policies that placed the public good in first position. Be that as it may, the two high street practitioners were elected as President and Vice-President, promising to shake up the Law Society. It was a disaster. Four of the top five staff, including John Hayes, resigned, and all were of such quality that they obtained better jobs elsewhere with ease. The Society totally lost credibility with the government. With a view to recovering from this nadir in its fortunes and to making the Law Society more efficient, 'reform' measures were determined on the basis of the advice of a leading businessman, brought in as a consultant. The Law Society, however, is not a business. Efficiency is not its sole or even its most important objective. To lead, the Society needs to carry the profession with it. It requires the participation and support of as many practitioners as possible. Taking power into the hands of a small group of office-holders, reducing the number of committees, and cutting down on the number of Council meetings, as advised, did make the decision-making process more efficient. It also made the Society more remote from the profession, and even from its own Council members.

The organisation headed for further trouble when Kamlesh Bahl became Vice-President. She was totally committed to the reform process and started to implement it in a 'hands on' manner. Staff made complaints about her management style, and Lord Griffiths, who conducted an independent enquiry, found against her. She was removed from office, but in such a manner that she sued the Law Society for discriminatory behaviour. The tribunal supported her plea, at least so far as the actions of the President (one of the populist candidates) and the Secretary-General appointed to replace John Hayes were concerned. It is only now, with Presidents chosen by the Council, that the Law Society is beginning to recover. It has much to do to gain any reputation with the profession, and even more to do to restore a measure of credibility with the public.

CHAPTER 13

The way we live now

Wih apologies to Trollope

When my time on the Council of the Law Society came to an end, I no longer needed to have a close association with a law firm and I also left Theodore Goddard. I had few regrets: a younger generation was coming to the fore in the firm, and I had little more to offer. I will, however, always be grateful for the way the firm took me in when I left IBM and needed shelter. For a couple of years I joined the London office of Triplet, a provincial French law firm based in Lille. I enjoyed it and was happy to help a French firm to establish itself in London. It had always seemed to me a pity that so few continental firms were prepared to expand outside their own country.

Now my sole remunerated activities are as a non-executive director of the Chelsea Building Society and of Océ UK, a Dutch reprographics company employing over 22,000, with a large UK presence of more than a thousand. My view of non-executive directorships was that they were easy money, reserved for the great and the good. However, I have found that, so long as I can avoid speaking up on every subject or attempting to usurp the role of the executive, I can help the management with advice based on experience at IBM. I never thought such directorships were for me, until I received a telephone call from Humphrey Sturt, whom I had known as a personnel manager at IBM. He had become a headhunter and said he was looking for a non-executive director for a major building society. I responded in the normal way by saying that I knew of nobody who could fit the role. 'No, Bill,' he said. 'It's you we want.' To thank him when I had been chosen, I took him out to lunch. 'Are there any more such jobs?' I asked. He said that there was one in a major reprographic company, but that the management wanted a technical specialist. I did not fit the profile and the shortlist of candidates had been submitted. Serving the wine liberally, I persuaded him to add my name to the list. The company concerned was Océ and I got the job. At the interview, the Managing Director commented that I was the only person on the list with the right background.

No other directorships ever came my way. I had thought that I would suit a French company, with major interests in the UK, or a British company with the equivalent in France. AGF, the major French insurance company, did offer a non-executive directorship in the UK, but then withdrew its offer, replacing it by a consultancy. I had discussions about a directorship or consultancy with Vivendi and with Kingfisher, but they came to nothing. This is not a cause for much regret. Even non-executive directorships take some time and I have a full and pleasant life. The computer has weaned me definitively away from attendance at offices. I find that I can work efficiently from home and sometimes wonder why I ever went to an office.

Soon after the deaths of Cécile, of Pitche and of her father André, the château at Belloy, the family home where we had been married, was sold. My mother-in-law, Simone, was most upset. I too regretted that there was no place where my children could feel a sense of belonging. So I bought, in their names, a house of their and Simone's choice and gave Simone the right to occupy it for her lifetime. I was careful not to go to see the house before I bought it, because I wished it to be their choice and not mine. Chloë thought that I was completely mad to buy a house unseen. However, the operation, if one can call it that, has been a success. The name of the house is 'Cap Horn' and it is not far from Belloy, at St Valéry sur Somme. Simone spends Christmas, Easter and the summer there; Odette, her sister, comes to stay; Koukla and her children join Simone during school holidays; my sons and their wives go to the house; and Chloë and I pop across from London for the occasional weekend. It takes under five hours to get there by car.[15] For a fortnight

15   Trips to Cap Horn do not count as 'skiing' holidays. In this context 'ski' stands for 'Spend Kids' Inheritance'.

in July, Oriana comes with her three children from Mexico. We call it the 'half way' house because it is easily accessible from both London and Paris.

The year after Pitche's death I married Chloë, Pitche's best English friend and the one time owner of Abercorn Place, the house we lived in when we first came to London from Paris. When Chloë agreed to marry me, I was surprised. I had known her for many years, but never thought that she liked me. In fact her son, James, tells a story about staying in the Château de Bormes with his mother when he was young. At the time, I was probably staying at Le Canadel along the coast. He asked Chloë what being a 'bounder' meant. 'Well,' she said, 'you know Bill Blackburn . . .'

Cap Horn in St Valéry sur Somme

Nancy Wise, the wife of Derek, my Theodore Goddard Paris boss, advised me to marry Chloë. I said that it was impossible, much as I admired her because, as she knew all about me, she would never accept me. Indeed, I did not think that she approved of me. Nancy said that I knew nothing about women, they were made of tougher stuff than men and that I would be surprised. She was right. I did ask her and she accepted.

My sons, her sons James and Oliver, and her daughter Oriana, all seemed happy, even enthusiastic, about this. Before the marriage took place, Oriana and Alexander invited us to go on a skiing holiday. When Chloë and I arrived, our children, with many giggles, showed us into a small room with bunk beds. After we had got married, Chloë asked what difference marriage would make to our lives. The first night we slept at Chloë's house in Alma Square. Oriana tapped on the door of our room and sat on our bed to chat. Next night we slept at my house in the New Kings Road. Alexander tapped on the door, came into the bedroom and sat on our bed for a chat. Neither would have done this, we agreed, if we had not been through the marriage ceremony.

Chloë has made me a happy man and I love her dearly. Sometimes she will admit that she is quite fond of me. This story is not about her, but I should record that she is the daughter of Sir James Gunn, the famous portrait painter. She is a gifted sculptor and one of the best cooks in the world. She had divorced her diplomat husband Sir Crispin Tickell several years before we married. Crispin, much decorated after a brilliant diplomatic career, went on to be the Master of an Oxford college. He is an expert on climatology and is often to be heard on the radio. One day our local butcher said to me that he had heard 'Chloë's husband' on the *Today Programme*. 'Brilliant, he was,' he said. I protested that Chloë was now my wife not Crispin's. 'Yes,' he said, musing. 'Sir Crispin – I suppose that if she hadn't married you, she'd have been a lady.'

Chloë's children and grandchildren are a great joy. All of a sudden, on marrying Chloë, my family grew. James, Oliver and Oriana have become almost my own. My sons were a little late in producing grandchildren. This did not matter so very much.

I had Phoebe and Alice, Sofia, Jaime and Miguel and, most recently, Anna Beatrice. As Sofia put it, 'Bill is not our grandfather you know, he just thinks he is.' Added to Koukla's children, particularly the loyal and loving Guillaume, I have a wonderfully wide and affectionate extended family. The rest will forgive me if I give pride of place to Sofia, who wrote the following:

> I hope you get well soon,
> I hope so all the way to the moon,
> I hope as high as the highest dune,
> That you will get well soon.
>
> I hope that you will get well now,
> Because without you life is foul,
> And life at home
> Without you is silent and boring as foam.

My sons Alexander and Jimmy know all about themselves and, as these reflections have been written for their benefit, I have not told their story. Perhaps, in due course, they will write their own memoirs for their children. However, for anyone else who may read this I would like to record a few things about my sons. I am proud of them both, and love and cherish them.

Alexander Peter Howard was born in Suresnes near Paris in 1963 and is a lawyer. Unlike me, he is a real international lawyer, qualified in both France and England. He is a partner in the leading corporate English firm, Slaughter and May, lives in Paris and works too hard. He is married to a Mexican, Carmen Maria Mariscal, known to everyone as Cari. Cari is a sculptor and her work takes the form of 'installations'. She designed a part of the Mexican Pavilion at the World Fair in Hanover and has given exhibitions, not only in Mexico but also in Barcelona, Madrid and Paris. They have twins – Julian William Nicolas and Maria Carmen Cécile.

Jimmy (James Alain Howard) was born in Abbeville near Belloy in 1965, and is

Chloë

the first DPhil in my family. I had said that he was the first in 'the' family but Chloë protested that her family had some PhDs. He is a specialist in Third World development and works as a consultant for the British and other governments and for international institutions, such as the World Bank. He lives in Peru with his Peruvian wife, Kathy, a medical doctor who specialises in public health. They have one child, André William Luis, named after Pitche's father, after me, and after Kathy's father. He is a gorgeous little boy: smiling, bright, energetic and intelligent, with black eyes and ivory skin, and a forceful character.

Because Alexander and Jimmy were born in France, their children would have had to have been born in the UK to inherit my British nationality. André was born in Bolivia, so he is Bolivian, Peruvian and French, but not British. The twins are just as exotic and are French, Mexican and American (because Cari was born in California and has US as well as Mexican citizenship). My children and grand-children have come a long way from my purely British origins.

This seems an appropriate place to end. Alexander and Jimmy, you have reproached me in the past for having spoken so rarely of my background. You said that you wanted to know more.

Now you know it all, or almost.

APPENDIX

Extract from *The Solicitors' Guide to Good Management*
(2nd Edition 2001)

COMMUNICATING EFFECTIVELY

1   NEVER PRESUME THAT A MESSAGE HAS BEEN UNDERSTOOD – test everyone's perception of a situation frequently:

> · when delegating, ask for instructions to be repeated;
>
> · when taking instructions from a client, repeat them in the course of the interview and at the end;
>
> · confirm all oral understandings in writing.

2   AVOID MEMO AND EMAIL WARS – if you are angry, never send a letter, memo or email to relieve your feelings; wait until you feel calmer and then talk about the matter with the person concerned.

3   AVOID WRITING SELF-INDULGENT LETTERS – these are the letters that give you more satisfaction than they give to the recipient (they almost always start with the word 'I'); write to confirm rather than to surprise and, above all, never send a bill that comes as a shock to your client.

4   KEEP EVERYONE INFORMED – spend some time deciding to whom you should send copies of each communication, and remember that information that informs one person may irritate another.

5   NEVER TELL A CLIENT THAT A MATTER IS GOING TO BE EASY – to do so may massage your ego and reassure the client initially, but when things, as they often do, turn out to be more complicated than at first foreseen, you will immediately lose your client's trust.

6 AVOID UNNECESSARY DEADLINES – if you miss a self-imposed deadline, your client will be disappointed: give yourself more time and be earlier than expected.

7 ASK FOR ADVICE AS FREQUENTLY AS YOU GIVE IT – temper your advice in the form of a question; even tough advice can be made more palatable if you seek your client's own advice and agreement.

8 GIVE BAD NEWS FACE TO FACE – we all have to break bad news; never put things in writing until you have spoken.

9 REMEMBER TO SAY THANK YOU – the easiest way to motivate people is to thank them. Of course, you must mean what you say – hypocrisy is easily recognised. Always remember that you yourself do not like to be taken for granted – neither does anyone else.[16]

16   If a third edition of this book should ever appear it will include a tenth point to the effect that, as people's capacity to take information on board is limited, one should normally, in an interview, inform a client of three facts, no more. This is an old general medical practitioners' adage, but it seems appropriate for lawyers.

Golden Oldies on the beach at St Valéry sur Somme